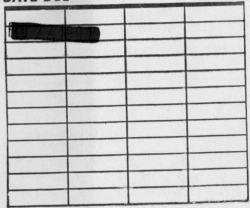

BECKETT AND THE VOICE OF SPECIES
A Study of the Prose Fiction

Eric P. Levy

BECKETT AND THE VOICE OF SPECIES

A Study of the Prose Fiction

GILL AND MACMILLAN
BARNES & NOBLE BOOKS
TOTOWA, NEW JERSEY

First published 1980 by
Gill and Macmillan Ltd
15/17 Eden Quay
Dublin 1
with associated companies in
London, New York, Delhi, Hong Kong,
Johannesburg, Lagos, Melbourne,
Singapore, Tokyo

0 7171 1021 4

First published in the USA 1980 by
Barnes & Noble Books
81 Adams Drive
Totowa, New Jersey, 07512

ISBN: 0-389-20004-2

Origination by Healyset, Dublin
Printed in Great Britain by
Redwood Burn Ltd.
Trowbridge & Esher

To Deborah

Contents

Acknowledgements

I wish to thank the following institutions and people: the Department of English and the Faculty of Arts of the University of British Columbia for granting me a one-year study leave during which the bulk of this book was written; Dr D. P. Kennedy and Mr J. Reynolds of Cambridge University for their help in making the magnificent resources of the Cambridge University Library available to me; my wife Deborah who, in addition to typing and discussing the manuscript, has given far more than any preface could declare.

Grateful acknowledgements are due to the following for permission to quote from Beckett's works: courtesy of John Calder (Publishers) Ltd for *Proust, Three Dialogues with Georges Duthuit, Six Residua, Murphy, Watt, Molloy, Malone Dies, The Unnamable, How It Is, Four Novellas, For to End Yet Again and Other Fizzles;* Calder & Boyars Ltd for *Mercier and Camier, Texts for Nothing;* Faber & Faber for *Our Exagmination Round his Factification for Incamination of Work in Progress;* Grove Press Inc. for *Murphy, Watt, Mercier and Camier, Three Novels, Stories and Texts for Nothing, How It Is* and *First Love and Other Stories;* Pan Books Ltd for *More Pricks than Kicks.*

Acknowledgements are similarly due to the following journals for permission to quote from my own previously published material: *ELH* for 'Voice of Species: The Narrator and Beckettian Man in Three Novels', 45 (1978), 343–358; *Mosaic* for 'Looking for Beckett's Lost Ones', Vol. 12, No. 3 (Spring 1979), 27–37; *Renascence* for 'The Metaphysics of Ignorance: Time and Personal Identity in *How It Is*', Vol. XXVIII, No. 1 (Autumn 1975), 27–37.

1

Introductory: The Pure Narrator and the Experience of Nothing

Predictions are tiresome but, when some future age seeks through literature to understand the experience of being human in our era, the works of Samuel Beckett will perhaps be consulted more than any others. In fact, the profundity of Beckett's works has hampered contemporary readers from reaching consensual interpretation of them for, still immersed in the context he explores, we cannot yet see clearly his vision of it. While the current population explosion of critics may sometimes seem to fragment our insight, this 'massive urge to supply an explanation', as Martin Esslin calls it,[1] arises from a growing need to tighten our grasp of a writer who expresses the predicament of being human common to us all. The outlines of agreement are now emerging after more than twenty years of preparation (the first critical study of Beckett was published in 1957 by Niklaus Gessner). As the responses of each new critic are superimposed on those of his predecessors, areas of overlap and complement are defined and from them a clearer notion of Beckett's significance to our age appears.

The aspect of Beckett's fiction exciting the most controversy is the preoccupation with self-consciousness. Critics have had great difficulty determining the appropriate frame of reference in which to understand the introspection of the Beckettian narrator. Is this self-consciousness primarily that of the artist trying to grasp his own creative act or is it that of a person withdrawing from the world of others either through insanity or sheer impotence?[2] In contrast, does this self-consciousness involve something more basic — an exploration of the very nature of self? If so, is this self to be construed in Cartesian, Hegelian, Kierkegaardian, Sartrian,[3] or

1

neo-Freudian[4] terms, to list just a few explanations attempted? Though conflicting, these interpretations recognise that in Beckett's *oeuvre* self and identity crack under the pressure of relentless scrutiny and that all the resources of our intellectual heritage must be gathered to excavate the rubble. In this study, I try to push the work a little further.

There is a passage in Samuel Beckett's *Three Dialogues with Georges Duthuit* which, unravelled, provides perhaps the shortest and most precise introduction to the severe world of Beckett's own prose fiction:

> The expression that there is nothing to express, nothing with which to express, nothing from which to express, no power to express, together with the obligation to express.[5]

This may seem a cryptic and unyielding utterance, but it is not so much an explanation as a First Principle which must be explained by the reasoning which led to it. In its immediate context, the passage suggests that contemporary art, denied traditional sources of material, has reached a dead end. There are no topics for it to explore that have not already been handled too many times by too many others. From this point of view, the phrase 'there is nothing to express' means 'there is nothing new to express'. But Beckett is driving deeper than this. Later in the same dialogue, he argues that art springs from the relation between two poles, the artist and the world that he sees. We can give these poles any names we choose, such as 'representer and representee',[6] 'perceiver and perceived', or 'self and world'.[7] As long as these poles are taken for granted and no demands that they be verified are made, all goes well. However, when the two terms on which art rests are themselves called into question, what is the artist to do? When each attempt to express explodes into a thousand questions about the self expressing and the world to be expressed, what is the outcome? Beckett has already given his answer: 'The expression that there is nothing to express . . .'

All art tries to illumine or clarify some part of human experience, and great art tries to grasp or even form the values guiding that experience in a given age. Before it can do so however, the poles of experience, subject and object, must themselves be stably defined. The interpretation of these poles changes from age to age but their intelligibility is never doubted. The point to grasp is that the ideas of self and world or subject and object are neither innate nor fixed. They evolve with civilization. The world posited by modern physics is not the same as the theological one painted by Raphael in *La Disputa del Sacramento*. Similarly, the *cogito* enunciated by Descartes is not the immortal soul endorsed by Plato nor is that soul, in turn, identical with the one described by Augustine. Yet, all three refer to the same subjective pole of experience. Beckett is reminding us that these poles of experience are not automatically intelligible; they must be constituted or defined by some set of assumptions, otherwise there can be no reference to them at all.

Far from discouraging him, this difficulty is the source of Beckett's inspiration, for he sees the inaccessibility of the two poles as *the* predicament of the human species in our time. The old Humanist tradition that for 2500 years articulated the special virtues of the species and developed a wealth of metaphysical and theological views about the ultimate significance of human experience has disappeared. In its absence, human experience of course goes on, but no longer has any means of taking stock of itself. In fact, there is no longer a clear idea of the species. No one explanation of human experience holds: is man, fundamentally, a soul in a vast universe of Being or an Ego in a private psychological world or a series of brain functions in a skull — the list continues indefinitely. Beckett explores human experience as he finds it today: denied any explanations but desperately needing them.

Like the artists and philosophers before him, he asks the question 'What does it mean to be human?' The answer he gets is disturbing: to be human is to seek endlessly for an identity and a universe in which to enjoy it. This is the plight of our species. Moreover, this position should in no way be construed as a brand of Existentialism or a doctrine of Absurdity. While these two other schools both address what they see as the fundamental contingency and perplexity of human experience, they nevertheless have no difficulty elaborately constructing the two poles, subjective or objective, of that experience. The doctrine of Absurdity, for example, puts man in a meaningless universe but does not hesitate to enumerate the characteristics of that universe nor to suggest ways for man to cope with life in it. Absurdity arises not so much from man questioning himself as from his interrogating the universe and adapting to its refusal to answer. In contrast, the questioning in Beckett's fiction no longer concerns merely the objective pole of experience (i.e. the universe), but now addresses the very process of structuring experience into the poles of subject and object. As Malone puts it, quoting Democritus out of context, 'Nothing is more real than nothing.'[8] Human experience is an experience of Nothing; the only reality it knows is the inability to interpret its own structure.

This, then, is the central idea in Beckett's prose fiction but its unfolding is a very gradual process. The experience of Nothing first appears in *Murphy* where precisely the same situation as that discussed in *Three Dialogues* occurs. Beckett is very explicit here. Murphy's vision, having literally no object, loses its subject as well. Two moments can be distinguished in this single act. First, experience has no object: '. . . Murphy began to see nothing, that colourlessness which is such a rare postnatal treat, being the absence (to abuse a nice distinction) not of *percipere* but of *percipi.*'[9] Next, that absence penetrates the subject: 'Murphy . . . continued to suck in, through all the posterns of his withered soul, the accidentless One-and-Only, conveniently called Nothing' (*Murphy*, 246). Thus, we have the beginning of an experience with neither subject nor object. It must be emphasised that this is only a beginning, for the experience of Nothing that Murphy undergoes is still framed by the familiar context of self and world. That is, the experience happens to an already constituted subject inhabiting a definite place. In Beckett's subsequent works, this familiar context is dropped and little by little, the experience of Nothing becomes the only context. Discovering how to express the experience of Nothing from within, with minimum dependence on any conventional means of presenting experience in terms of subject and object, is perhaps Beckett's greatest triumph. He accomplishes this feat by making first person narration express the absence of these two poles. It is all a matter of boldly exploiting the very structure of narration.

The most obvious observation to be made concerning first person narration is that it rests on two terms: a narrator and the story he tells. Customarily, far more stress is placed on the story than on the narrator whose primary function is, after all, simply to tell one. Yet, as every reader of Beckett has noticed, the primacy of story over narrator is progressively reversed in Beckett's prose fiction. More and more in each text, the narrator draws attention to himself at the expense of his story until he becomes the most important part of his narration. Thanks to the number of cross-references, repeated phrases, and revealing statements throughout Beckett's prose fiction, many readers have made a second observation: each work is told by the same narrator whose reason for telling or trying to tell stories never varies. Finding this single narrator in the works preceding *The Unnamable* is not always easy for often, as in *Molloy* or *Malone Dies,* he hides behind the named personae through whom he seeks to express who he is. The central problem for us will be to explain the identity of this narrator and to discover how, through him, Beckett creates a symbol for the vacancy of human experience.

Right from the start with *More Pricks than Kicks,* we become aware that a very peculiar kind of narrator is at work, one who wants to tell a story not so much to entertain or instruct an audience as to set up a persona through whom he can hint at his own lack of identity. From *Watt* on, the narrator uses narration as a more and more obvious means of reflecting the questions about self and world that define his own experience. By *The Unnamable,* the personae drop away and these questions so inundate the narration that the story and the act of telling it are one and the same; the narrator can only speak of his need to know who is speaking: 'Where now? Who now? When now?' (*Unnamable*, 291). Thus, Beckett makes the two terms of narration — narrator and story — converge. The Beckettian narrator knows only the endless experience of trying vainly to complete the narrative act. In many of the works, he does appear to be telling stories of some real or imagined past like any other narrator, but on closer inspection we find that each tale is an elaborate device by which he is actually expressing his lack of any experience other than the interminable one of struggling to narrate. In fact, the Beckettian narrator is so driven by the obligation to narrate that he may best be called a pure narrator; that is, his whole being is contained in the act of trying to tell a story. He has nothing else to fall back on.

This is quite a change from the conventional first person narrator who is bolstered by a host of assumptions from which Beckett excludes the pure narrator. Let us consider what these assumptions are. From his first words, we accept the conventional first person narrator as an intact and recognisable self who, like us, has an existence outside the act of narrating. To go further, the essence of selfhood, that which creates for us the illusion of his selfhood, is his ability to narrate, in the present, the story of his experience in the past when he was not narrating. Even if the narrator begins referring to his very act of writing or talking, the assumption that we are listening to a fellow self — one who has a past and present independent of the narrative act which describes them — still holds. The pure narrator, in contrast, is not a self or a person with a past apart from the act of narration; he cannot tell of a time when he was not speaking: 'never anything but lifeless words'.[10]

Furthermore, from the reader's point of view, the conventional narrator appears to have a choice about narrating; the decisions to start and end seem to be entirely his own. The pure narrator, however, cannot make the same easy transition from his private world to the world of narration, because for him the two are identical. He *is* only in so far as he narrates. Hence, we find scattered throughout the prose works references to the impossibility of making a proper beginning: 'It would help me, since to me I must attribute a beginning, if I could relate it to that of my abode' (*Unnamable*, 296); 'How can I go on, I shouldn't have begun, no I had to begin,' (*Texts*, 75). Neither is there a shortage of references to the difficulty of making an end: 'you must go on, I can't go on, I'll go on,' (*Unnamable*, 414), 'it's for ever the same murmur, flowing unbroken, like a single endless word and therefore meaningless, for it's the end gives the meaning to words,' (*Texts*, 111). In short, the pure narrator can do nothing but narrate his need to narrate, nothing but tell stories of his desire to have that need no longer.

At this point a paradox emerges. The more the narrator talks, the more he is aware of the silence that surrounds him and which he must overcome if his task is ever to end: 'I'm shut up, the silence is outside,' (*Unnamable,* 410) or 'there is only silence,' (*Texts,* 139). Narrating the need to narrate ultimately means talking about the silence which the narrative act is trying to break: 'The silence, speak of the silence before going into it . . . at every instant I'm there, listening to me speaking of it . . .' (*Unnamable,* 407). What do these paradoxes signify? Beckett is uncovering the fundamental assumption underlying all narration. The first thing any narrator must have before he can tell a story is a context in which to be heard. Just as all external and distracting noise must be kept out if we are to understand music as music and not as mere sound, so in narration all other words must be stilled before the narrator can be heard. To put it another way, narration, like any other art, fundamentally involves two poles: expression and the silence or stillness from which expression arises and without which it would be unintelligible and unnoticeable.

Conventional narration, precisely because it implies a larger world from which the narrator withdraws in order to tell his story, guarantees or assumes the relation between these two poles; neither the reader nor the narrator has to worry about it. Indeed, it is the existence of the larger world that creates the need to establish this polarity in the first place; otherwise, as we have seen, there would be no way of protecting the narrative world from the disruptions and distractions of the larger one we all share. In pure narration, however, the situation is not at all the same, and we can best understand why by performing a little experiment. Take any conventional first person narrator and, at the very moment he begins his story, have him forget everything but that he must narrate. He is now a pure narrator who cannot simply tell a story and resume his private existence, because he no longer has any existence except through narration. He has been thrown into the narrative world with no hope of emerging again and no memory of ever having been in any other world.

What, then, is his experience in this universe of pure

narration? To begin with, the narrator is now no more than a bare expressive pole with nothing to speak of but his relation to the other pole of narration — the silence. If we continue the experiment, we shall find that the narrator's relation to the silence soon breaks down and that, even worse, so does his relation to the expressive pole. Unable to maintain his relation with either pole of narration, the pure narrator is stranded between both, with absolutely no way to resolve his predicament. His burden is always to question and never to reach an answer; he has no means of grasping his own experience.

If the narrator has only his relation to the silence and no way to determine his own boundaries, how can he know where he ends and the silence begins, how can he separate himself from the silence he is experiencing? Questions like these abound in *The Unnamable:* 'I feel no place, no place round me, there's no end to me' (*Unnamable,* 399): 'The silence, speak of the silence before going into it, was I there already, I don't know, at every instant I'm there, listening to me speak of it, I knew it would come, I emerge from it to speak of it, I stay in it to speak of it . . .' (*Unnamable,* 407). The narrator cannot be sure whether the silence remains external or whether, from moment to moment, it is internalized as a hiatus or lapse in his own being: 'I'll know I'm silence, no, in the silence you can't know, I'll never know anything' (*Texts,* 112).

It would seem, of course, that to fix his relation with the silence the narrator has simply to speak of it and so fulfill his function as expressive pole. But if he does this, his very recourse to words contradicts the relation he seeks to confirm. By using words to clarify his relation to the silence, the narrator unhappily creates another problem: how can he claim his own words if they will not do his bidding? Try as he might, he can never make words express his experience of the silence, for the only way to express silence is to be silent. But, if he stays silent he has no way to identify himself in the silence, no way not to become one with the silence, no way, quite literally, to be himself. Hence, the narrator must always speak of the silence, but be forever estranged from his own words, his own voice. Again, *The Unnamable* is strewn with references to the defection of words and the narrator's inability to claim the voice speaking them: 'there is I, on the one hand, and this noise on the other...' (*Unnamable*, 388); 'in the end you don't know anymore, a voice that never stops, where it's coming from' (*Unnamable*, 369); 'I'll speak of me when I speak no more' (*Unnamable*, 392).

This is the impossible situation of the pure narrator. In order not to disappear in the silent pole of narration he speaks, but by speaking he is divorced from the expressive pole of narration — words or the voice using them. What we have now is a narrator lost between the two poles of narration which alone condition his experience. He knows that there must be some relation between these two poles, words and silence, but he cannot relate himself to that relation: '... it has not yet been our good fortune to establish with any degree of accuracy what I am, where I am, whether I am words among words, or silence in the midst of silence. . . .'[11]

The pure narrator, then, is the means Beckett has found to express the experience of Nothing, a flux of empty experience with neither subject or object. In fact, to the extent that it implies a discrete self discoursing upon a definite world of experience, the term, 'narrator', is misleading. The frequent use of the first person pronoun, 'I', far from denoting such a discrete self, is merely part of the effort to fix some subjective pole to the flux of empty experience: '... it's the fault of the pronouns, there is no name for me, no pronoun for me, all the trouble comes from that...' (*Unnamable*, 404). Often, the same tactic is used in reverse when the narrator denies being the 'I' the narration is trying to refer to. If he is not this 'I' then he must at least be another as yet unidentified one. The disclaimer, 'It's not I', recurs in almost every work after *Malone Dies*. Finally, the biggest clue to the absence of any subjective pole or self appears in the narrator's repeated references to the purely passive nature of his utterance and his claim to be merely recording what another voice is muttering. The phrases, 'I say what I hear' and 'I say it as I hear it', are especially prominent in *The Unnamable, Texts for Nothing,* and *How It Is*. Here, Beckett has hit upon a perfect way to indicate the absolute passivity of the experience of Nothing where empty impressions are registered but with no definite subject responsible for having them in the first place.

Thus, in the pure narrator and his experience of Nothing, Beckett expresses the impasse reached by the great enterprise of Western Humanism. With Beckett, as throughout this tradition, the ultimate task of self-consciousness is to know oneself *qua* man; that is, to decipher in the contours of personal experience the trace of species in us all. Interpretations of this trace have never been constant, and more theological eras have seen it as rooted to an Absolute or participating in God. For Beckett, the trace of species appears in the need to structure experience and fix the poles of self and world. The real Fall occurred not in Eden but in our century. After the accumulation of too much history, we have lost the innocence required to believe in any more explanations. The only certainties left are the falseness of all interpretive structures and the radical unintelligibility of human experience without them.

2

More Pricks than Kicks and *Murphy:*
Birth of the Beckettian Narrator

There are few journeys in literature more beguiling than the long, uncertain one launched by the Beckettian narrator looking for himself. Failure makes his labours no less engaging, so ingenious is their strategy. With each successive story, he completes another circuit, trying relentlessly to reach the centre his revolutions imply but cannot touch. That centre, where he hopes to be, is never more than a structural hypothesis like the thousands built by the narrator in the course of his wanderings. Like those myriad hypotheses, it dissolves upon close inspection leaving, instead of a centre, the nagging need for one. The unique triumph of Beckett's prose fiction is this communication of an experience without a definite centre, an experience that has lost contact with the limiting poles of self and world.

In his first two novels, *More Pricks than Kicks* and *Murphy,* Beckett creates the framework that will support the great explorations in his later texts. *More Pricks than Kicks* inaugurates the reflexive technique characteristic of all Beckettian narration. We are given a narrator who tries to mirror his own emptiness through the feeble attempts of his persona, Belacqua, to evade the demands of personal identity. This is the genesis of a closed narrative system excluding everything but the void at its centre. In *Murphy,* through a complex arrangement of mirrors, Beckett expands that central void to envelop every aspect of narrated experience.

Some bibliographies prefer to list *More Pricks than Kicks* — a reworking of a much longer, unpublished novel, *Dream of Fair to Middling Women* — as a collection of ten stories rather than as a novel.[1] The distinction is a nice one for, though the ten chapters are readily separable into short stories (and, indeed, two were later so treated), their cross references and sequential handling of the protagonist, Belacqua Shuah, entitle the work to be called a novel. Belacqua himself, as befits the first of a long line of Beckettian characters, cuts a sorry figure. In the bloom of young manhood, he is a myopic, fat, short, balding Dubliner prone to rashes and aching feet. Even worse, the narrator gives him little opportunity to rise above the restrictions of his unusual name. Like Dante's Belacqua, he succumbs to indolence and daydreaming; like Er and Onan, sons of the biblical Shuah, he seems to have a predilection for the effusion of semen in vain, especially following voyeuristic escapades. Yet, the greatest restriction of all, and the one which his sloth and cowardice make it impossible to escape, is life itself. Despite careful planning and a willing female accomplice, Belacqua botches his one suicide attempt so badly that the narrator cannot refrain from clucking his tongue: 'Who shall judge of his conduct at this crux? Is it to be condemned as wholly despicable?'[2] In fact, Belacqua's repeated attempts to evade the burdens of his own subjectivity are matched only by his incompetence in carrying any of them through, and for this good reason the narrator calls him the 'inept ape of his own shadow' (p. 36). By the time of his death, Belacqua has pretty well forfeited any remaining claims to selfhood.

No doubt Belacqua is an exasperating creature. He wants to live in his mind, but too often yields to the various demands of the body. Moreover, indolence prevents him from making his mind a worthy place in which to dwell. Too lazy to stock it with his own ideas, he steals from others, making them 'his own' (p. 146). On the one occasion when he ventures an original contribution, it turns out to be Bruno's old notion of the coincidence of contraries, duly transcribed by Beckett himself in his first published essay: 'Indeed he even went so far as to hazard a little paradox on his own account, to the effect that between contraries no alternation was possible' (p. 148). This kind of appropriation seems innocent enough until we remember Belacqua's solipsist ambition. By sparing his own thoughts and incorporating those of others, he risks eventually inhabiting a mental world with no personal mind. The Unnamable's inability to claim his own 'I' shows just how grave the consequences of such negligence can be in Beckett's universe. Compounding the problem, Belacqua strives at times to discard mind altogether by letting the body usurp its functions. This tactic, involving random sallies whose only destination is ultimate return to their point of departure, he calls 'gression', and in this way body mimes the mind's 'aptness to receive . . . the faint inscriptions of the outer world' (p. 36). Belacqua has obviously read his Locke a little too enthusiastically, and his impulse to make every action imitate the movement of the mind only aggravates the difficulty of determining whose mind it is.

Belacqua is given a last chance to confront the responsibility of an individual mind and fails miserably. This occurs in the chapter, 'Yellow', where he languishes in a hospital room, awaiting the removal of an anthrax from his neck. Belacqua is terrified at the possibility of death on the operating table, but refuses even to admit that the fear is for himself, pretending instead to be concerned about his family's reputation: 'But the unfortunate part of it was that this would appear in his behaviour, he would scream and kick and bite and scratch when they came for him, beg for execution to be stayed and perhaps even wet the bed, and what a reflection on his late family that would be!' (p. 146). The word, 'behaviour', is a significant one in the passage, for right up until the moment he dozes under the anaesthetic Belacqua tries to tailor his every gesture and word to what he thinks are the expectations of the doctors and nurses who comprise his audience. This is not so much vanity as a distraction from *timor mortis*. He cannot bear the thought of his own death, because he has always been unwilling to think for himself. The contemplation of death necessarily involves an examination of who one is in life, and Belacqua is clearly disqualified from such introspection. His sloth is precisely the desire for some torpid state between life and death.

To the surprise of everyone, Belacqua actually does die on the operating table. His sudden death is obviously parallel to the lobster's abrupt demise at the end of the first chapter, 'Dante and the Lobster', and a consideration of that earlier death will help us understand the significance of Belacqua's termination in the evolution of Beckettian fiction. Quaking at the sight of his aunt dropping the unfortunate crustacean into boiling water, Belacqua thinks: '. . . it's a quick death, God help us all' (p. 19). The narrator's immediate contradiction, 'It is not', is rich in implications. This is not simply a knowing correction from an omniscient narrator whose interjections remain in the same context or world as the characters he chides. Rather the contradiction has such abrupt and categorical authority that it draws us away from the narrated world in which Belacqua makes his incorrect statement and impels us toward a different world from which that statement is negated.[3] In other words, as with Moran's famous disclaimer at the end of Molloy, 'It was not midnight. It was not raining,' we begin to see that in Beckettian fiction the narrated world is ultimately important only in so far as its contradiction implies quite another world of experience otherwise incommunicable.

On a preliminary level, the narrator's contradiction moves us into the death agony which seems interminable to the lobster but remains closed to anyone outside it. But we can go further than this. Since the lobster's 'quick death' prefigures Belacqua's death in the later chapter, we are impelled, when finally reading of this character's unexpected end, toward his silent torment as well. Moreover, since Belacqua, as we shall see next, is merely a reflection of his narrator, it follows that Belacqua's implied death agony can become a means of approaching the narrator's own predicament. This technique will be fully exploited in *Malone Dies*. By *The Unnamable* the Beckettian narrator will go beyond the confusion of dying and employ the metaphor of damnation in 'this hell of stories' in order to express more and more completely his own vacant experience.

In the closed narrative system of *More Pricks than Kicks,* Belacqua has no substance apart from the narrator's comments on him which in turn must inevitably rebound upon the narrator himself, since it is upon him that Belacqua's existence depends. When complaining, 'He was an impossible person in the end. I gave him up in the end because he was not serious,' (p. 36) the narrator indirectly admits this responsibility. Repetition of the phrase, 'in the end', suggests that Belacqua's sudden death under ether owes more to the narrator's attitude toward his creature than to the incompetence of the anaesthetist. The narrator, moreover, shares the lack of seriousness for which Belacqua is reproached.[4] Notice how flippantly he speaks about his story: 'This may be premature. We have set it down too soon, perhaps. Still, let it bloody well stand' (p. 59). The narrator even admits to writing occasionally in Belacqua's style which further reduces the distance between them: '. . . the reader is requested to take notice that this sweet style in Belacqua's' (p. 41).

While pushing Belacqua so harshly through adventures to a sudden death, the narrator is careful, as he will be throughout the Beckettian canon, to stifle any pity for his persona. There is good reason for this strategy. By responding with the same compassion to any misfortune, pity sees only piteous objects and never truly confronts the private worlds of suffering subjects. To treat Belacqua's world, the narrator must keep it apart from all others, and this means banishing pity which otherwise tends to assimilate every private world into a single, common one. In fact, the first chapter, 'Dante and the Lobster', develops a fable on the topic.[5] The narrator divides the story into four distinct sections: Belacqua struggling with the second Canto of the *Paradiso,* preparing lunch, enjoying an Italian lesson, and finally watching his aunt boil the unfortunate lobster. Each of the sections treats the same theme — pity or mercy for the damned or condemned. The first, labouring over Beatrice's explanation of the 'spots on the moon', suddenly thrusts forward the old belief which Beatrice tries to replace: 'the spots were Cain with his truss of thorns, dispossessed, cursed from the earth, fugitive and vagabond. The moon was that countenance fallen and branded, seared with the first stigma of God's pity, that an outcast might not die quickly' (p. 11). The second intrudes the leitmotiv more subtly. While preparing lunch, Belacqua notices a newspaper photograph of McCabe, an assassin condemned to die the next morning: '. . . the Malahide murderer's petition for mercy, signed by half the land, having been rejected, the man must swing at dawn in Mountjoy and nothing could save him' (p. 15). The third broadens the scope of pity to include the damned. Belacqua's tutor, Signorina Adriana Ottolenghi, advises: ' "It occurred to me," she said, 'apropos of I don't know what, that you might do worse than make up Dante's rare movements of compassion in Hell" ' (p. 16). The last section, as we have seen, evokes Belacqua's pity for the doomed lobster.

Closer inspection reveals that each of the four sections deals with misguided pity. In the first, God's pity for Cain is a 'stigma', because it prolongs his persecution. In the second, pity for the murderer, McCabe, might encourage more murders elsewhere. In the third, Virgil himself, in a passage quoted by Belacqua, repudiates Dante's pity for the damned: 'Qui vive la pietà quando è ben morta' (p. 16). Belacqua's pity for the lobster involves the same error for which Virgil reproves Dante: pity for the justly condemned only adds wrong to wrong. Indeed, the narrator draws an explicit parallel between the couple of Dante and Virgil and that of Belacqua and his aunt by comparing Belacqua's entry into his aunt's kitchen with Dante's descent into Hell. Even Virgil's embrace of Dante is repeated: 'She embraced him and together they went down into the bowels of the earth, into the kitchen in the basement' (p. 18). These four proscriptions against misguided pity point in each case to an impenetrable suffering that must somehow be grasped on its own terms and not translated into others more familiar and diluted. This principle of impenetrable suffering dominates the later chapter, 'Yellow'. Had the narrator there treated his character with the same pity that Belacqua directs toward the lobster, the hermetic world of Belacqua's suffering would have seemed porous and accessible. Yet, as shown, the narrator is at pains to seal Belacqua off from our common world so that, at the moment of this character's death under ether, the reader glimpses an absolutely closed world of experience whose centre has been in the process of disappearing throughout the novel. When we remember that Belacqua has no substance apart from the narrator he reflects, it becomes clear how with *More Pricks and Kicks* Beckett takes the first big step toward creating a completely closed narrative system inhabited by a narrator trying to express his own peculiar experience — one which, as we shall see in Murphy, is an experience of Nothing.

Murphy, Beckett's next novel, clearly concerns a series of closed systems, each telescoping into the next and all enclosed by Murphy. First there is the closed system of astrology, wheeling the stars and planets into places, establishing the general chronology of the novel, and pushing Murphy closer and closer toward fatal isolation. This last they only seem to do, however:

> The more his own system closed round him, the less he could tolerate its being subordinated to any other. Between him and his stars no doubt there was correspondence, but in Suk's [his astrologer's] sense. They were *his* stars, he was the prior system (pp. 182–3).

The more Murphy's system asserts itself, the more visible will appear any others that reflect it. Thus, astrology appears most influential as precisely the moment when Murphy's own system is declaring its independence. Similarly, the second closed system, that constituted by the figures surrounding Murphy, resorts most to Murphy when he has decided to resort only to himself. In this system, the need of each character for another forms an unbroken chain such that the changing of one character's needs involves an immediate and corresponding change in the others. Neary, quoting his former pupil, Wylie, grasps this from the individual's perspective:

> The syndrome known as life is too diffuse to admit of palliation. For every symptom that is eased, another is made worse. The horse leech's daughter is a closed system. Her quantum of wantum cannot vary (p. 200).

Eventually, all the supporting characters need Murphy who is just entering the peace of his own closed system:[6] 'Murphy then is actually being needed by five people outside himself' (p. 202).

As Murphy, the 'seedy solipsist' (p. 82), recedes more definitely into himself, the number of closed systems reflecting him increases. Each inmate at the insane asylum, Magdalen Mental Mercyseat, where he works for seven days and one night before breaking all ties, inhabits a closed system. Murphy is delighted:

> Except for the manic . . . the impression he received was of that self-immersed indifference to the contingencies of

the contingent world which he had chosen for himself as the only felicity and achieved so seldom (p. 168).

The most charming patient is Mr Endon, a schizophrenic whose inner world no one can penetrate. One unfortunate night, he defeats Murphy in a game of chess and, profiting from his opponent's resultant stupor, slips from his cell to play with the light switch outside the hypomanic's compartment. During neither game can Mr Endon's moves be fathomed. He acts 'in a way that seemed haphazard but was in fact determined by an amental pattern as precise as any of those that governed his chess' (p. 247). He seems literally to incarnate a closed system. Later, Murphy finds Mr Endon and leads him back to bed. Like the other closed systems in the book, Mr Endon is a reflection of Murphy – in this case literally. Peering into Mr Endon's protuberant eyes, Murphy sees '. . . in the cornea, horribly reduced, obscured and distorted, his own image' (p. 249). From what we have seen so far, then, Murphy is located at the centre of concentric closed systems which, one and all, reflect him. Locked in this hermetic universe, Murphy has access to himself only as reflected object, never directly as subject. This he recognises:

> The last Mr. Murphy saw of Mr. Endon was Mr. Murphy unseen by Mr. Endon. This was also the last Murphy saw of Murphy (p. 250).

Beckett is marking a significant advance here. While remaining on the level of conventional characters inhabiting a conventional world (more or less), Beckett is clearly creating a narrative context that has collapsed into one experiencing centre which, as we shall see later, is not so much a centre as a perspective on the void. The other characters, the other worlds (astrological, amatory, and insane) are important only through signifying Murphy whom they enclose with multiple reflections of his own absent self or subjectivity. In fact, as shall eventually be shown, Murphy contains the whole universe of *Murphy;* everything outside him in the narrative universe of this novel reflects him.

The model for this extraordinary narrative structure is Leibnitz's theory of monads. Some connection between

Leibnitz and Murphy has already been observed by critics since Beckett drops some obvious hints in the text.[7] Murphy's garret at the Magdalen Mental Mercyseat is described in terms that clearly echo the *Monadology:* 'The compartment was windowless, like a monad, except for the shuttered judas in the door . . .' (p. 181). In Beckett's later French translation of *Murphy* (Paris: Editions de Minuit, 1947), the reference is strengthened through the mention of an earlier period when, in Hanover, Murphy actually inhabited the same garret where Leibnitz lived and died: '. . . Murphy avait occupé à Hanovre assez longtemps pour faire l'expérience de tous ses avantages, une mansarde dans la belle maison renaissance de la Schmeidestrasse, où avait vécu, mais surtout où était mort, Gottfried Wilhelm Leibnitz' (p. 119). Finally, the connection begins to gain the force of an identification when we note that, at the end of the novel, Murphy dies in his garret at the Magdalen Mental Mercyseat.

According to Leibnitz, the universe is a closed system created by God and containing an infinite number of monads or perceiving atoms. Each monad has the faculty of perception and from its particular position in the universe reflects or represents all the others. No two monads, therefore, perceive the same thing and the only monad that perceives the whole universe with perfect clarity is God — the central monad. All the others perceive with a degree of clarity corresponding to their proximity to God. There is no interaction among monads. The perception that each enjoys is due to an internal principle and not to external causes. That is, God has so ordered the universe in pre-established harmony that each monad, locked within itself and with 'no windows through which anything may come in or go out',[8] will perceive or, more precisely, represent to itself successively all the changes of perception occurring in every other monad. Since each monad is thus a mirror — from its own position — of all the other monads, the universe becomes a vast system of reflections of itself.

Beckett's application of Leibnitz to *Murphy* will now be clear. The Leibnitzean system of monads, each reflecting a universe created by God at the centre, becomes a narrative system of 'puppets' (p. 122), each reflecting Murphy at their centre. The novel thus comprises a series of monadic mirrors of Murphy's own solipsistic universe. There is a peculiarity in Leibnitz's monadology which Beckett exploits for his own purposes. As the great historian of philosophy, Wilhelm Windelband, has pointed out, the Leibnitzean universe has no real content. Each monad in it is defined, not by any intrinsic properties, but by its relation to all the others — that is, by the way it mirrors all the others:

> The monad *a* represents the monads *b, c, d, . . . x.* But what is the monad *b?* It is in turn the representation of the monads *a, c, d, . . . x.* The same is true for *c*, and so on *ad infinitum.*[9]

Hence, we have a system of relations but cannot say anything about the terms being related. It is a universe of empty relations. Windelband's critique, it should be noted, would pose no problems for Leibnitz, since according to him God enjoys, by definition, absolute content and has created the monadic universe to mirror that content in the fullest way possible. But remove God and the Leibnitzean universe becomes a hall of mirrors which seems to contain a centre but which in fact contains nothing.

This, of course, is exactly what Beckett does in the novel. Beckett surrounds Murphy with narrative mirrors which, even as they seem to confirm him, are actually reflecting — as Mr Endon does explicitly — Murphy's lack of any definite centre. Murphy directly experiences this inner void during his celebrated vision of Nothing which immediately precedes his examination of Mr Endon's eyes. The passage, already briefly considered in our Introduction, must now be quoted in full:

> . . . Murphy began to see nothing, that colourlessness which is such a rare postnatal treat, being the absence (to abuse a nice distinction) not of *percipere* but of *percipi.* His other senses also found themselves at peace, an unexpected pleasure. Not the dumb peace of their own suspension, but the positive peace that comes when the something give way, or perhaps simply add up, to the Nothing, than which in the guffaw of the Abderite naught is more real. Time did not cease, that would be asking too much,

but the wheel of rounds and pauses did, as Murphy with
his head among the armies continued to suck in, through
all the posterns of his withered soul, the accidentless One-
and-Only, conveniently called Nothing (p. 246).

The initial phase of Murphy's vision is simply the immediate
and literal result of his solipsism: he sees *nothing* outside
himself. The second phase is the paradoxical consequence of
the first. If there is nothing outside the self, then there can be
no self at all; for the self can exist only in relation to a world
or not-self to which it is opposed. Hence, Nothing begins to
enter Murphy as well: '. . . Murphy . . . continued to suck
in, through all the posterns of his withered soul, the accidentless One-and-Only, conveniently called Nothing.'[10]

By thus taking solpisism to its logical conclusion, the
vision of Nothing breaks down the Leibnitzean closed system
of mirrors which provided Murphy with illusory reflections
of a self that was not really there at all. When these distorting
mirrors shatter, Murphy plunges into an experience involving
not merely the absence of world, as in solipsism, but also the
absence of self. Freed at last from the false testimony of
mirrors, the experience of Nothing is also, as the passage
insists by invoking Democritus of Abdera, a vision of Reality:
'. . . to the Nothing, than which in the guffaw of the Abderite
naught is more real.' Murphy's experience of Nothing is of
archetypical importance in Beckettian fiction; all the subsequent texts will explore new ways of expressing it. The high-
est truth to which human experience can aspire is the encounter with its own void and the recognition that every
attempt to circumscribe experience by some explanatory
system only constructs more mirrors which falsely reflect a
centre or a meaning that, in reality, can never be found.

The vision of Nothing would not be possible without long
preparation, and this is provided by Murphy's frequent trips
to the celebrated third zone. The third zone quite obviously
offers an escape from the burden of subjectivity. Otherwise,
Murphy would not rock his way there so eagerly:

Here there was nothing but commotion and the pure forms
of commotion. Here he was not free, but a mote in the
dark of absolute freedom. He did not move, he was a point

in the ceaseless unconditioned generation and passing away
of line (p. 112).

The passage insists that there is little difference between
Nothing and the third zone: 'Here there was nothing but
commotion and the pure forms of commotion.' Take away
the commotion and you are left with Nothing. But where do
these forms of commotion come from? The answer is not far.
The narrator's account of the third zone and the two zones
below it draws heavily on philosophical terminology, especially that associated with Scholasticism. We find terms like
'in intellectu', *'in res'*, 'becoming', 'forms'. A strong memory
of the Platonic doctrine of Ideas also appears: 'Perhaps there
was outside space and time, a non-mental non-physical Kick
from all eternity . . .' (p. 109). In fact a more serious attempt
is made here than anywhere else in Beckett's prose fiction to
pin down in formal terms the experience in question. The
echoing of these metaphysical schools recalls their doctrine
of an intelligible universe containing pure forms apprehended
only by the intellect or mind. Now the ascent from the first
to third zone repeats the same ascent made in classical philosophy from imperfect levels of knowledge to the perfect
realm of intellectual truth. The narrator carefully stresses
that the third zone is the zone of mind *par excellence*. The
first two zones, fantasy and contemplation respectively, are
imperfect in so far as both depend in their movement upon
extraneous factors. The first zone must react against the
physical world whose frustrations it reverses; the second is
contingent upon Murphy's choice of objects to contemplate.
The third zone, in contrast, is truly the intelligible zone, concerned exclusively with 'pure forms'. Since the third zone
has already been identified as the closed system of Murphy's
mind, the forms it contains can relate only to that mind. The
third zone is, in short (with apologies to Aristotle), Murphy's
mind thinking itself, apprehending the pure forms of its own
structure. Yet, these pure forms are the opposite of those
envisaged in classical philosophy. In the old schools, 'form'
designates that which does not change, but here it refers to
endless change or becoming — precisely that which has no
form. In thinking itself, Murphy's mind attempts to appre-

hend intelligible forms but can find no genuine ones. The best it can do is to give intelligible form to its own vacancy. This is the origin of the 'pure forms of commotion'.

At this point, it becomes clear that the third zone and the vision of Nothing are two aspects of the same system. The vision of Nothing, perceiving no object at all, eventually accepts the presence of Nothing in the perceiving subject. As a direct intuition of the Real, it involves no thinking or intellectual act, and to this extent resembles mystical revelation. In the third zone, on the other hand, the mind, in thinking itself, thinks the Nothing which it contains and, in so doing, gives Nothing intelligible form, for that is the way the mind knows. The forms of commotion, in other words, are the endless attempts of the mind to find some meaning to the void in which it thinks.

We have found that every closed system in the novel is a reflection of Murphy and that Murphy himself gets lost in the Nothing that fills his own closed system. We can go further and establish that every detail in the narration is a reflection of Murphy and the abandonment toward which he tends. The main supporting figures mirror him so clearly that at times we seem to be looking at two versions of the same subject. Compare these passages. First Mr Kelly with Celia:

> She halted — 'Get away!' said Mr. Kelly — set herself off in the line that his eyes must take on their next declension and waited. When his head moved at last, it was to fall with such abandon on his breast that he caught and lost sight of her simultaneously. He did not immediately hoist it back to the level at which she could be assessed in comfort, but occupied himself with his sheet. If on his eyes' way back to the eternities she were still in position, he would bid them stay and assess her (p. 13).

Then Murphy with Celia:

> When Murphy found what he sought on the sheet he dispatched his head on its upward journey. Clearly the effort was considerable. A little short of half way, grateful for the breather, he arrested the movement and gazed at Celia. For perhaps two minutes she suffered this gladly, then

with outstretched arms began slowly to rotate . . . like the
Roussel dummy in Regent Street. When she came full
circle she found, as she had fully expected, the eyes of
Murphy still open and upon her. But almost at once they
closed, as for a supreme exertion, the jaws clenched, the
chin jutted, the knees sagged, the hypogastrium came forward, the mouth opened, the head tilted slowly back.
Murphy was returning to the brightness of the firmament
(pp. 13—14).

The second passage repeats the first with minor alterations.
Mr Kelly's bed sheet becomes a sheet of paper, his 'eternities'
become the stars. Later on we hear that, like Murphy, Mr
Kelly even owns a favourite chair, although in his case it is a
wheel-chair. Moreover, in his strong physical resemblance to
Mr Endon (both men have deep eye sockets, protruding eyes,
little bodies, and big heads), Mr Kelly reflects Mr Endon who
in turn reflects Murphy.

Celia too mirrors Murphy as far as differences of sex and
temperament allow. She develops an irresistible desire to be
bound naked in Murphy's chair and even enjoys her own version of the third zone in it:

She closed her eyes and was in her mind with Murphy, Mr
Kelly, clients, her parents, others, herself a girl, a child, an
infant. In the cell of her mind, teasing the oakum of her
history. Then it was finished, the days and places and
things and people were untwisted and scattered, she was
lying down, she had no history (pp. 148—9).

At the coroner's inquest, only the sudden recollection that
'her solitude was not without witnesses' (p. 269) prevents
Celia from tearing the envelope containing Murphy's will.
This duplicates Murphy's decision 'mindful of his memory,
and that he was not alone' (p. 93) not to rip the envelope
containing his horoscope. Celia's acquisition of a double
in the 'old boy' upstairs to the point of adopting, after his
suicide, both his apartment and pacing habits, mirrors the
way Murphy is reflected in his own 'old boy', Mr Kelly.

Narration mirrors Murphy in other ways. Murphy's holding
Celia's wrists while sprawled in bed discussing her future with

him repeats Mr Kelly's same gesture while treating the same topic from his own bed. Much later, Celia will recline on Murphy's bed while discussing Murphy with Neary, Wylie, and Counihan. There are, finally, several narrative reflections of Murphy's abandonment and death. The closed system of Neary and Company breaks up, its dispersal mirroring the scattering of Murphy's ashes on the pub floor. Mr Kelly, by collapsing after losing his kite when the line snaps, engages a whole battery of mirrors. The kite is once described as a 'speck' (p. 25) and later soars into the 'unseen' (p. 280). Hence, Mr Kelly's kite is a speck in the unseen just as Murphy, reflected in Mr Endon's eyes, is a 'speck in Mr. Endon's unseen' (p. 250). The phrases echo the third zone where Murphy is a 'mote in the dark of absolute freedom' (p. 112), and reveal the tremendous risk of staying too long in it: one may remain there permanently. Mr Kelly's abandonment over his errant kite duplicates Murphy's before Mr Endon. In neither case will the tiny speck ever be seen again. Celia provides a concluding reflection of this abandonment but in more conventional terms. The closing words 'All out', called by the park rangers refer also to Celia, reminding us that she is at the end of her emotional tether, wheeling home her stricken grandfather, Mr Kelly, and mourning Murphy. With her last gesture, she enters her own version of the unseen: 'She closed her eyes' (p. 282). This is the same phrase used to describe the entry into her own third zone: 'She closed her eyes and was in her mind with Murphy, Mr Kelly, clients, her parents, others, herself a girl, a child, an infant' (pp. 148–9).

The book, then, is concerned far less with Murphy as one character than with the construction of a closed narrative system everywhere reflecting the abandonment or absence on which it rests. Every element in the novel either reflects Murphy or reflects other elements which in turn reflect Murphy who is, 'turn and turn about' (*Molloy*, p. 70), just a means of reflecting the experience of Nothing. The narrator has only to step forward, as he will in the later novels, and reveal that he built this narrative system in order to reflect his own strange experience in it and thereby gain some expression of his identity. Not before *The Unnamable* and *Texts for Nothing* will the narrator make such a confession, but the impulse is already present in the first two novels. With a confidence that seems easy now but was surely remarkable for an unknown writer embarking on such a difficult journey, the young Beckett drafts the narrative universe which will later serve his narrator so well.

The risk Belacqua takes in forging a mental world with no personal mind is paid for in the second novel where Murphy, like Mr Kelly's kite, wanders too long in his zone. Narration for The Unnamable will be a bewildered attempt to express an experience which unfolds in no place or time, with neither subject nor object. It will be a direct extension of Murphy's third zone, an experience always aware of its own movement but bare of any meaning:

> I'm in words, made of words, others' words, what others, the place too, the air, the walls, the floor, the ceiling, all words, the whole world is here with me, I'm in the air, the walls, the walled-in one, everything yields, opens, ebbs, flows, like flakes, I'm all these flakes, meeting, mingling, falling asunder, wherever I go I find me, leave me, go towards me, come from me, nothing ever but me, a particle of me, retrieved, lost, gone astray, I'm all these words . . . (*Unnamable,* p. 386).

If Murphy could speak from the third zone, after the vision of Nothing has floated away whatever remains of his personal identity, that is what he would say.

3

Watt: Narration and the Problem of
Subjectivity

The critical response to *Watt* shows clearly that in grappling
with Beckett's fiction we are also boring down to the impasse reached by contemporary thought. The effort to understand Watt's own struggle to understand the perplexing abode
of Mr Knott has led critics to seek assistance from two different intellectual movements in our own age which have
wrestled with the problem of determining meaning. The first
of these is Logical Positivism. Since Jacqueline Hoefer first
linked the names of Watt and the early Wittgenstein whose
Tractatus Logico-Philosophicus became the central document
of Logical Positivism, one group of critics — primarily English
and American — have argued that in this novel the central
character struggles to establish objective truth in a world
refractory to rational analysis.[1] According to this view, Watt
wanders around Mr Knott's residence rather like a frustrated
Logical Positivist trying desperately to use the two key intellectual tools of his trade: first, that what cannot be expressed by means of logical propositions does not exist, and
second that what is expressed can have meaning only if it can
be verified. If an expression or proposition cannot be verified,
if, more precisely, the proposition has no conditions for
verification at all, then that proposition means nothing.
Justus Hartnack in his lucid study of Wittgenstein elaborates:

> It is not due to some shortcoming in me or anybody else
> that no meaning can be found; there is none to find, noth-
> ing to be known; the proposition is meaningless.[2]

Watt's failure to make verifiable statements about the world
of Mr Knott becomes the failure — or perhaps the nemesis —
of an entire philosophical movement. By pitting Logical

Positivism against a situation that defeats it, Beckett is able, these critics seem to imply, at once to enunciate his own position and to reveal that position as the *cul-de-sac* toward which modern thought has inevitably tended.

The second major critical approach to *Watt* draws on what is perhaps the leading intellectual movement today: structural linguistics. To understand this new view, whose key sources are such works as F. de Saussure's *Cours de linguistique générale* and Emile Beneveniste's *Problèmes de linguistique générale*, let us return to Logical Positivism for a moment. According to Logical Positivism, the task of language is to depict what is already in the world, what is already real. To discharge this task without including meaningless propositions that have no connection with reality, language must employ only propositions that can be verified by empirical observation of the world. Now, what structural linguistics finds inadequate here is the assumption that the function of language is simply to express what is already there in the world, what is already real. According to structural linguistics, language has no 'objective validity', if by that phrase we mean that language can actually point to something real unaffected by it. Reality is linguistic; that is, our very notion of the world is already structured by language. The intelligibility that we think belongs to the world derives instead from the way we talk about the world. We cannot prevent the relations between words that make language intelligible from infiltrating the reality we hope to elucidate by means of language. Expression is caught in a paradox. Only through words can there be meaning, but that meaning relates ultimately only to the words which express it.

Two French critics, Olga Bernal and Fernande Saint-Martin, refer to this principle of structural linguistics when interpreting Beckett's fiction.[3] Olga Bernal, for example, sees Watt's predicament as a kind of post-structuralist yearning for a place where naïve faith in the power of language to explain external phenomena can once more be satisfied: 'There is nothing as disturbing in modern literature as Watt's nostalgic desire again to seize language and prevent it from failing him.'[4] Just as Adam was the first man to name the animals, Watt becomes the first man to inhabit a world beyond the reach of language, a world encountered through sense perception only and that will not conform to any concepts or verbal structuring.

While it is obvious that these two critical views — the one applying Logical Positivism, the other, structural linguistics — help illumine *Watt,* there is much concerning the presentation of experience in this novel that they overlook. To begin with, both views regard Watt as a discrete and fully constituted subject in direct relation to an external world, however vague and confusing. But to do so is to beg the fundamental question of Watt's own independence, his own ability to distinguish himself from his bewildering experience. Before treating Watt's attempt to verify his own statements or even to make statements at all, the problem of his own identity must be solved.

The opening of the novel is illuminating in this regard. Instead of treating Watt, the first scene concerns Mr Hackett, a reasonably genial hunchback who, after successfully dislodging a pair of lovers from his bench by charging public indecency, is himself disturbed by an acquaintance, Mr Nixon, and his spouse. The narrator drops out during the ensuring dialogue, because he is not needed. Dialogue always presupposes a shared world of events and communicable assumptions, and Mr Hackett, despite his hunch and eccentricity, is still a part of it. Such is not true of Watt, however. When he suddenly appears, alighting from a bus before it has reached the designated stop, two of the conversing characters gaze at the stranger in uncomprehending amazement, while the third, Mr Nixon, crosses the street to talk briefly with him. But Watt is so far beyond the world of familiar assumptions that Mr Nixon's interference, far from shedding light, only increases his uncertainty about Watt: 'I tell you nothing is known, cried Mr. Nixon.'[5]

Under these conditions, it is not at all easy to move from the known world to Watt's private one, yet this very difficulty will provide a means. Watt is so accustomed to abuse as an impenetrable and ridiculous object in the world of men that he no longer reacts to others. The first axiom of his own private world is exclusion from any public one. When Lady McCann beans him with a stone, Watt ignores the affront:

'For it was an attitude become, with frequent repetition, so part of his being, that there was no more room in his mind for resentment at a spit in the eye, to take a single example, than if his braces had burst . . .' (p. 32). Watt's initial tendency, then, as subject is to take for granted his role as abused object. He does not notice being noticed; he expects it. But let Watt feel unnoticed, unwitnessed, for one moment, and he grows uneasy. Very early in his journey, he responds restlessly to the moon: '. . . he felt the moon pouring its now whitening rays upon him, as though he were not there. So, settling his hat firmly on his head, and reaching forward for his bags, he rolled himself over into the ditch, and lay there, on his face . . .' (p. 33).

Watt's dependence on witnesses is revealing. The function of any witness is to verify some perceived event or object, and a witness can do this only by locating that event or object in some already established context. The Apostles, for example, can witness a miracle as a miracle only by placing the event in a context or world where miracles are possible. Hence, for Watt to be witnessed is for him to be located in some definite context, to be put into a stable relation with the external world. But, on the other hand, if Watt is not witnessed or, as with the moon, if he feels ignored by a witness, then he has no assurance of his relation to the outside world. His efforts, as we shall see, to forge that relation on his own usher in an even bigger problem: the struggle to explain his experience of the outside world generates the new experience of seeking that explanation. The longer this secondary experience continues, the farther it takes him from the primary one he is trying to explain and, even more important, the more it begins to confuse or merge with his experience of himself, his subjectivity. It is not hard to see what is happening here. Without witnesses, Watt faces the same peril as Murphy: the loss of a stable relation to both the objective and subjective poles of experience. In other words, without witnesses, Watt will enter the experience of Nothing.

This is precisely the case as soon as Watt crosses the threshold of Mr Knott's house. Watt tries, as with the famous incident of the piano-tuning Galls, to construct the context or stable objective pole that seems missing in his experience. But he fails because every guess can be replaced by another in an infinite chain. Before long, such reflection, inventing what was never present, becomes itself a new experience: 'To such an extent is this true, that one is sometimes tempted to wonder, with reference to two or even three incidents related by Watt as separate and distinct, if they are not in reality the same incident, variously interpreted' (p. 78). In short, Watt cannot separate what he is experiencing (i.e. the objective pole of his experience) from his attempts to determine what he is experiencing, his attemps to establish the objective pole.

Like Murphy in the third zone, Watt has entered an experience of pure flux, relating to nothing but itself and itself nothing but the pure form of experience with no content:

> Thus the scene in the music-room, with the two Galls, ceased very soon to signify for Watt a piano tuned, an obscure family and professional relation, an exchange of judgments more or less intelligible, and so on, if indeed it had ever signified such things, and became a mere example of light commenting bodies, and stillness motion, and silence sound, and comment comment (p. 73).

In this experience where 'nothing had happened' (p. 76), the polarity between subject and object fades away. Thus, reflection as an act by a subject upon its own experience is impossible. No longer a reflexive return of a subject to its experience, reflection becomes the recurrent return of the same experience to that subject: '. . . it revisited him in such a way that he was forced to submit to it all over again, to hear the same sounds, see the same light, touch the same surfaces, and so on, as when they had first involved him in their unintelligible intricacies' (p. 76). We can see that the distinctions blur between outer and inner, as Watt is reduced to a finite centre around which the experience flows. He is not so much a self as merely the place where experience is registered.

In order to reassert his subjectivity, Watt must somehow turn 'nothing had happened' into 'something had happened', and the only way to do this is by those finical hypotheses for which he is so notorious. With them, Watt is trying not to establish fact or the disposition of the outer world (we have seen the infinite series such an attempt costs him) but to preserve himself by shoring up the old distinction between subject and object that the witnessing of nothing has destroyed. Unfortunately, hypotheses are verbal formulations, and Watt has trouble with the very words which form them. In Mr Knott's house where experience is about itself alone, where nothing happens but the pure forms of perception (movement, contrast, etc.), words have no definite objects to name; ultimately, their only function is to bolster, the subject uttering them. Watt's celebrated struggle with the pot that refuses to be called, 'pot', is a good example. No objects seen in or from Mr Knott's house will 'appear in their ancient guise' (p. 84), for the very principle of appearance — the relation of an object to a finite subject — has disappeared in the general welter of *nothing* happening. Experience no longer respects the distance between self and things:

> Things and himself, they had gone with him now for so long, in the foul weather, and in the less foul. Things in the ordinary sense, and then the emptinesses between them, and the light high up before it reached them, and then the other thing, the high heavy hollow jointed unstable thing, that trampled down the grasses, and scattered the sand, in its pursuits (p. 84).

The use of the word, 'thing', when referring to both object and pursuing subject indicates that the only dependable distinction between them is that pursuit. Subjectivity is always problematic in Beckett, and Watt's predicament is an excellent example. Beyond the pale of ordinary experience, Watt deploys words in an effort to restore the lost polarity between subject and object. He seeks not to know but merely to continue as a subject until and if he can end.

In Erskine's room hangs a picture that represents Watt's problem geometrically: a circle, open at the bottom, occupying one plane, a centre outside the circle occupying another. At first sight, the two seem to be seeking each other: 'a circle and its centre in search of each other . . .' (p. 129), but this statement generates a series of alternatives concluding with 'a circle and a centre not its centre in search of a centre and a circle respectively, in boundless space, in endless time. . . .' The drawing is rich in implications. Imagine two circles and, beside them, two centres. How are we to know to which circle each centre belongs? The question no longer sounds gratuitous when we identify each circle or circumference with the boundaries of a familiar world of experience and each centre with the proper subject of that experience. How horrible for a thinking centre to find itself suddenly in the wrong circle or, worse, in no circle at all, and to know it can never rest until reaching the right one. Arsene, during his long welcoming address, tells Watt of just such a transformation:

> The sun on the wall, since I was looking at the sun on the wall at the time, underwent an instantaneous and I venture to say radical change of appearance. It was the same sun and the same wall, or so little older that the difference may safely be disregarded, but so changed that I felt I had been transported, without my having remarked it, to some quite different yard, and to some quite different season, in an unfamiliar country (pp. 43—4).

Once this happens, how long will it be before the centre forgets what a centre is?

This is what the pursuit of subjectivity means to Watt. If the only way to remain a centre is to be inside the appropriate circumference, then the centre in this situation must constitute its own circle, bounded by the limits of its own imagination. It is easy to observe, then, how the picture is a symbol or mirror of Watt's search for himself amid bewildering experience, but the picture is also the occasion of this search. Watt cannot separate his experience of the picture from his hypotheses about it. His experience generates hypotheses, but these can never explain his experience. They plunge him headlong into an infinite regress: Watt seeks the meaning of a picture whose meaning in turn, as we have seen, is his own search for an explanation, his own quest for a context in which he can find himself. Beckett is driving the point home with characteristic emphasis.

There is one scene near the end of the novel where the

hypotheses drop out, and Watt's comprehension keeps pace with his experience. His term of service ended, he passes one night in the waiting-room of a train station in order to buy a ticket the next morning. Strangely serene, it is the still centre of the novel for, unlike Mr Knott's house, the waiting-room provides a context with certain boundaries, and even harbours one object in addition to Watt to guarantee the equilibrium between self and world: 'But that little was enough, for Watt the possibility was enough, more than enough, that something other than he, in this box, was not intrinsic to its limits' (p. 234). During his vigil, darkness deepens then lightens to reveal very slowly a chair and later a picture of a horse. Like the incident with the Galls, this is a case of 'light commenting bodies', but the similarity goes no further. At the station, Watt's experience concerns the appearance of light and bodies in a room, a definite context, very different from the appearance of bare experience which is what we found the Galls to signify.

The demand for context, for a stable relation between self and world, differs from the demand for clarity, and the confusion of the two is responsible for the unholy union of Watt and the Tractatus Wittgenstein mentioned earlier. Watt never carries his inquiry beyond appearance into the reality or verification of the object: 'For Watt's concern, deep as it appeared was not after all with what the figure was, in reality, but with what the figure appeared to be, in reality. For since when were Watt's concerns with what things were, in reality?' (p. 227). As his placidity in the waiting-room testifies, he is perfectly content to see an object vaguely as long as the context sanctions that vagueness. Otherwise, he tumbles into the frustration of seeing a vague object, and that is insupportable. Consider this example. A little before entering the waiting-room, Watt watches a figure of maddening ambiguity toiling toward the station, making no headway. Until he dismisses the object as a hallucination, it elicits a torrent of hypotheses ('Or, if it was a nun, that it was not a man, or a woman, or a priest, dressed up as a nun,' p. 227) and a violent impatience. It is the context (road, approach, laws of perspective) that makes Watt demand clarity. Elsewhere, he would be, as he is in the waiting room, happy with obscurity.

We have established, then, that Watt needs his hypotheses only when there is a breakdown in the relation between self and object such that the context no longer tells Watt what he is experiencing. The story of Watt's tenure at Mr Knott's is the story of hypotheses grappling with the confusion of this experience of Nothing. The myriad hypotheses build a structure that seems of independent solidity but which everywhere points to the empty flux it tries to order. Like the appetite of Mary the parlour maid, experience knows 'no remission' (p. 52). Every instant must be worded, lest all cling together in the same void. Complaints about the loose structure of *Watt* miss the point; for in such a world, narration, desperately trying to make distinctions in a perfectly homogeneous flux, can no more determine the correct sequence of incidents than can a geometer decide from which of an infinite number of points on the circumference to draw the diameter of a circle.

Mr Knott will illustrate. He is not a genuine character, but merely an ideal limit or point of reference in Watt's empty experience. There is no way of separating him from the flux of which he is the postulated centre. He too is that mindless flux. When Watt finally encounters him in the garden, his employer passes unseeing, breathing like 'a child asleep' (p. 146). Since this is their only meeting, we never have any evidence that Mr Knott is anything more than a convenient way for Watt of representing and focusing his own confusion. Mr Knott's 'physical appearance' (p. 209) regularly changes, and Watt never arrives at any 'conception' (p. 120) of him whatsoever; for concepts must abstract from experience and here there is *nothing* for the mind to carry away. In watching Mr Knott who cannot be extricated from 'the long supposition' (p. 131) about him, Watt is actually witnessing his own efforts to order his experience, to create an object of that experience. By these meagre means, he preserves his subjectivity.

Having come this far, we must also see that the plight of Watt trying to order his own experience of Nothing comprises only a part of the novel. As with *Murphy,* Beckett is not content merely to narrate the experience of Nothing, but wants that experience to engulf every aspect of the narration. In *Murphy,* as he have seen, the entire narration becomes a great system of mirrors reflecting the void at its centre. In *Watt,* Beckett goes a step further and makes the act of narration an attempt to preserve the two poles of self and world in the midst of an experience of Nothing which over-whelms them. This he accomplishes through refining the mirror device used in *Murphy.* The novel presents Watt not as an independent character but rather as a mirror image of the narrator behind him.[6] During one interlude, the narrator (who calls himself 'Sam') allows mirror images to prolifer-ate: '. . . then we began to draw ourselves forward, and up-ward, and persisted in this course until our heads, our noble bulging brows met, and touched, Watt's noble brow, and my noble brow' (p. 155). These culminate in an explicit refer-ence: '. . . I felt as if I were standing in front of a great mirror . . .' (p. 158). Watt and the narrator soon break into a *pas de deux,* and the detailed description of their embrace makes it obvious that the narrator is dancing with his reflec-tion.

The mirror motif is extremely revealing. Through Watt, the narrator is trying to reflect an image of himself or, more accurately, his difficulty in conjuring such an image. Watt's plight in constituting the objective pole of his experience is, in turn, a reflection of the narrator's attempt to constitute his own subjective pole. To understand this relation, consider what happens when any subject looks into a mirror: he be-holds himself as a reflected object. That is, the act of reflec-tion turns the subject into an image, an object. The same law obtains in *Watt:* to reflect the effect of the experience of Nothing on his subjectivity, the narrator must project an image of the effect of that experience on objectivity. Hence, he gives us Watt floundering at Mr Knott's. Not before *The Unnamable* will the Beckettian narrator find a means of ex-pressing directly the loss of individual subjectivity in the ex-perience of Nothing.

With each new novel, Beckettian narration expresses more seriously the absence of subjectivity that the experience of Nothing entails. Though the narrative mirrors in *Murphy* all point to a central emptiness, the novel still takes subjectivity for granted in ways that no longer apply to *Watt.* In *Murphy,* the absence of subjectivity begins as a pleasant diversion from the cares of mind and body. To attain it, Murphy simply enters a contemplative state he calls 'the third zone', relegating fantasy to the first zone far below. The third zone is still a limitable experience which Murphy can enter almost at will (or, more precisely, when he suspends his will). Yet, at no time does his subjectivity completely disappear. The narrator's description of Murphy's third zone contains an apparent contradiction whose explanation will prove this statement. On the one hand, Murphy is fixed: 'He did not move, he was a point in the ceaseless unconditioned generation and passing away of line' (*Murphy*, p. 112). On the other, he hurtles: 'But how much more pleasant was the sensation of being a missile without provenance or target, caught up in a tumult of non-Newtonian motion' (pp. 112–113). From an external viewpoint, Murphy as the subject of this unusual experience is stationary. From Murphy's viewpoint, however, he does move, for, immersed in the experience of movement, he too seems mobile. Obviously Murphy's subjectivity is sufficiently intact for the narrator to take these two different points of view on it. Even more important, the third zone as a lived experience has not yet expanded to fill the entire narrative universe; there is still a point of view outside it.

All this changes with Watt through whom the narrator reflects a more complete image of his own bewildering experience. Watt is plunged directly into the chaotic experience of Nothing that characterises the third zone but, unlike Murphy, it is now the only experience he knows. Murphy's exhilarating dalliance with 'the flux of forms, a perpetual coming together and falling asunder of forms' (*Murphy*, p. 112) becomes for Watt at Mr Knott's a 'coming and being and going in purposelessness' (p. 58) and 'the approaches and separations' of 'a purely plastic content' (pp. 72–3). The experience is new to Watt so he asks only about the objects before him, but by *The Unnamable* the questions will be aimed at the subject undergoing that experience: 'Where now? Who now? When now? Unquestioning. I, say I. Unbelieving' (*Unnamable*, p. 291). We can understand why this happens by recalling the description of Murphy's third zone:

'But how much more pleasant was the sensation of being a missile without provenance or target, caught up in a tumult of non-Newtonian motion.' The word 'sensation' here suggests the impression of movement a passenger in a stationary train will have when another train moves past his window. Progressively in Beckett's fiction, the third zone or experience of Nothing becomes a prison in which the narrator or his persona, looking through the bars of his own vacant and rushing experience, is locked from the stillness of his own subjectivity.

4

Mercier and Camier: Narration, Dante and the Couple

Beckett kept his third novel, *Mercier and Camier,* on the shelf for twenty-five years before reluctantly allowing its French publication in 1970. The book was apparently more valuable to him as an exploration of expressive forms than as a work of art in its own right. Indeed the novel is clearly a kind of pivotal exercise, for here we can see Beckett on the one hand stressing the type of futile dialogue he was to perfect a few years later in *Waiting for Godot* (the French edition was published in 1952), while on the other hand further developing the system of narrative mirrors so useful in *Murphy* and *Watt* for expressing the experience of Nothing.

We do not have to read very far into *Mercier and Camier* to discover that the story as much concerns the narrator as the two eponymous heroes. With the first sentence the narrator thrice intrudes the first person pronoun, founding his own subjectivity on the adventures of the two characters: 'The journey of Mercier and Camier is one I can tell, if I will, for I was with them all the time.'[1] In recounting the futile existence of his characters, the narrator is somehow trying to grasp his own, but the attempt remains unsuccessful for their vain wandering only mirrors his confusion. They cannot understand their journey because it has been imposed upon them, and the narrator is improvising as he goes along: 'So let him wake, Mercier, Camier, no matter, Camier, Camier wakes. . . . Why? No knowing. No knowing such things anymore' (p. 103).

Under these severe circumstances, how can the characters preserve the narrator who so exploits them? Part of the answer appears in Beckett's brief article on the painter, Henri Hayden. There, in phrases that illumine his own work as much as his immediate topic, Beckett looks beneath the rubble of collapsed conventions for the last safeguard and testament of subjectivity, and finds it 'quite simply in the saving of a relation, a separation, *a couple,* however impoverished the components: the I with its possibilities of acting and receiving, the rest in its docility as the given' (my translation and italics).[2] The couple, of course, has become a renowned institution in Beckett's fiction, and Mercier and Camier (the novel was written around 1945) are its first representatives. The couple's function is to protect subjectivity by assuring its relation to a world by which it is bounded, any world, even that of its own torment or solitude. Such, for example, is the relation between Hamm and Clov in *Endgame.* Hamm is the centre whose world of experience Clov confirms and defines. But Mercier and Camier have their roles less well differentiated, and for this reason The Unnamable later calls them a 'pseudo-couple' (*Unnamable,* p. 297). Both are subjects; each props up the other so that together they may inhabit a world in which subjectivity — their own and the narrator's — persists. Sometimes the task is more than they can manage: 'And there were times they would look long at each other, unable to utter a word, their minds two blanks' (p. 17).

The world they inhabit is their journey, and that journey boils down to a question about purpose: 'What were they looking for?' (p. 23). Subjectivity, then, knows itself only as a striving to know what it is doing and who it is. Here Beckett reduces the polarity between self and world to its simplest form: the endless bumping of self against the walls of its own ignorance. The walls at least confirm its independent existence. The only truth ever revealed to Mercier and Camier involves the same paradox that runs through all of Beckett's works — the need to have a need is all that keeps the subject going: 'Finally a great light bathed their understandings, flooding in particular the following concepts. There are two needs: the need you have and the need to have it' (p. 72). Needs, by pointing to a deficiency in the subject, always imply a world outside where they can be gratified. In Beckett's reflexive universe where the subject turns more and more tightly in upon himself, the external world has been completely lost, and need now refers to the worst deficiency of all — the need for continuous proof of personal existence in a world of others.

This proof comes fitfully and negatively to Mercier and Camier and only when witnessing or causing the death of some other, as the fat lady or the constable. Death is the unique event in this redundant universe, the sole thing that, happening but once to a given individual, can confirm his individuality. All other acts and occasions are cyclic, recurring endlessly, varying only according to local circumstance. Consequently, the reaction of Mercier and Camier to each of the two deaths they behold is significant. The first restores Camier's will:

Let this be a lesson to us, said Camier.
Meaning? said Mercier.
Never to despair, said Camier, or lose faith in life (p. 33).

The second convinces Mercier that he and Camier live as two different subjects each of whom needs the other to remain a subject: 'We would never have hit on it alone, said Mercier' (p. 94). Each makes the other's relation to the world a little more secure. These restitutions are fleeting, however. Eventually, the two separate and recede into darkness.

The narrator emphasises that the journey is in search of subjectivity by modelling it upon the greatest itinerary of the soul in Western Literature: Dante's *Divine Comedy*. It is not so much a case here of *Mercier and Camier* paralleling or mimicking the *Divine Comedy* as of the later work being superimposed upon the earlier spiritual voyage. Hence, at every moment we can see, underneath the wanderings of this Beckettian couple, the Dantean convictions which they cannot even glimpse. The gap between the two works makes *Mercier and Camier* at once pathetic and pointless, for the couple retain Dante's earnestness ('Men less tenacious might not have withstood the temptation to leave it at that,' p. 71) but have lost all notion of goal or end. Imagine Dante and Virgil traversing Hell, Purgatory, and Heaven a thousand times, with no memory of their entrance, no hope of an exit, no means of judging those they meet, and no way of evaluating their own experience. Eventually, the stage would be reached where there is nothing in Dante to distinguish

him from Virgil and vice versa. That is the starting place for
Mercier and Camier. Unlike Dante's, their journey is morally
neutral. At various points, as we shall see, they slip directly
from Hell to Paradise with no increase or remission of their
suffering. Most of the novel, however, relives the *Purgatorio,*
because it is here that we can best gauge the utter futility of
their striving. As our discussion will show, Mercier and
Camier can make no progress; they pass no fewer than four
times through the same purgation for the same sin. Yet, they
are not the only ones thus ensnared. With them we shall find
the narrator in various disguises, for he is vainly attempting
the greatest purgation of all — release from the need to go on
searching for his own subjectivity. After charting the connec-
tions with the *Divine Comedy,* we shall be in a position to
consider how the novel is superimposed upon another world
as well: Beckett's narrative one stretching all the way back to
Murphy. Against this double background, the narrator of
Mercier and Camier will yield even more of his secrets.

The first chapter opens, as we might expect, with a strong
echo of the first Canto of the *Inferno.* Where Dante, overcome by fear of three predatory beasts, does not at first
recognise Virgil whom Beatrice has sent to guide him, Mercier
sees 'in the morning mist a shape suggestive of Camier's'
(p. 8), but it takes forty-five minutes for them to remain long
enough in the same place finally to meet. Instead of moving
Mercier and Camier steadily forward from this point in Hell,
the rest of the first chapter projects the couple against the
background of the *Purgatorio,* placing them sometimes in the
Earthly Paradise at the summit of the Mountain of Purgatory,
sometimes at its base, near the entrance to Hell. The implication is clear: wherever the couple wander they always remain
in the same unresolved situation. The 'small public garden'
(p. 9) where they greet each other is dominated by a single,
enormous tree which recalls not the entrance to Hell, but
the Earthly Paradise just above Purgatory. There (Canto
XXXIII), the forbidden tree is an immediate symbol of
divine Goodness: 'Whoso robs that tree or rends it offends
with blasphemy an act against God . . .'[3] With Beckett it
becomes just another item progressively desecrated in the
endless round of corruption and generation: 'The stifled

giant's days were numbered, it would not cease henceforward to pine and rot till finally removed, bit by bit' (p. 10). Another little detail derives from this part of the *Purgatorio*. From time to time in the novel, Mercier makes rather cryptic utterances that cannot be explained by the immediate context but which come directly from the *Divine Comedy*. The first of these occurs in Chapter I: 'A drunken woman passed by, singing a ribald song, and hitching up her skirts' (p. 13). This apparition duplicates that of the 'ungirt harlot' Dante spies in the Earthly Paradise (Canto XXXII). Mercier and Camier are far worse off than the lowest of Dante's damned, for their universe admits of no redemptive or structuring principle. Indeed, the little garden is invaded by two copulating dogs, echoes of the beasts that menace Dante. Even here, Mercier and Camier feel the presence of the damned of the First Circle whose sighs are the first Dante hears: 'I sense vague shadowy shapes, said Camier, they come and go with muffled cries' (p. 19). The ranger who disturbs the couple and surveys their eventual departure, 'his bunch of keys in his hand' (p. 20), recalls the warder at the gate of Purgatory who holds the keys given him by St Peter. Since we cannot tell whether Mercier and Camier are leaving or entering Purgatory when they quit the garden, the first chapter has succeeded in suspending all notions of direction or end, retaining only that of indifferent movement.

Chapter II, gathering and blending elements from each of the three cantos, grinds away the last hope of a definite conclusion to a journey that can by now mean nothing. The strangely silent crowd that buoys Mercier and Camier along the town streets recalls the 'shadowy shapes' intuited by Camier in the previous chapter. Yet, before we can trace their descent deeper into Hell, the couple reach a crossroads that abruptly returns them to Purgatory. Camier's question, 'Which way do we drag ourselves now?' (p. 42), echoes the first Terrace (Canto X) where Virgil and Dante lose their bearings. Camier's follow-up remark, 'Then let us turn back', explicitly contradicts the warder's warning in the previous Canto of the *Purgatorio:* 'Enter, but I bid you know that he who looks back returns outside.' The confusion over the 'mixed choir' (p. 25) that Camier hears and Mercier dismisses as a 'delusion' duplicates the debate Dante holds with himself on the First Terrace (Canto X), trying to decide whether or not he hears singing: 'In front people appeared and the whole company, divided into seven choirs, made two of my senses say, the one: "no", the other: "yes, they sing" . . .'

After this, the Dantean references shift even more swiftly. Mercier, in a fit of rage, smashes the malfunctioning umbrella and curses God: 'And to crown all, lifting to the sky his convulsed and streaming face, he said, As for thee, fuck thee' (p. 26). Here two Cantos are compressed. The beating rain belongs to the Third Circle of the *Inferno* (Canto VI), but the great malediction is hurled much later in Canto XXV by the thief, Vanni Fucci, who shakes his fists: 'Take that, God, for at Thee I square them!' A few lines later, with no transition, Mercier and Camier stand inside Helen's apartment. This is Paradise and she is Beatrice. The connection with Beatrice will grow clearer later on, but we can note now the ease with which Mercier and Camier enter and leave her domain. She can offer them only diversion, not permanent repose, and certainly not vision. The ailing cockatoo languishing in the room, its feathers 'blazing in ironic splendour' (p. 27), is a sorry version of the Eagle of Divine Justice, 'preening its feathers' in Canto XIX of the *Paradiso*.

The next morning the couple resume their wanderings and their journey, far from unfolding confidently, is whirled cruelly against three of the most significant moments in the *Purgatorio*, shattering any vestiges of purpose or meaning. The fatal accident involving the fat woman recalls the collision of the ecclesiastical chariot and the eagle in Canto XXXII. Mercier's delighted reaction — quite the opposite from Dante's response to this vision of lingering weakness in the Earthly Church — borrows from the last lines of the *Purgatorio*, where Dante, cleansed in the River Eunoe, emerges 'remade': 'Ah, said Mercier, that's what I needed, I feel a new man already' (p. 33). The remark is a hollow one; a few lines later the chapter ends with Mercier passing one hand over his rain-soaked face: 'He had not had a wash for some time' (p. 34). Here we are transported back to the opening of the *Purgatorio* where Virgil, wetting his hands with dew, washes the grit of Hell from Dante's cheeks. Life

itself is Purgatory for Mercier and Camier who do again and
again what they have already done, what they can never do
for good.

Chapter III begins deceptively. The first person voice
recounting its childhood seems, through almost two pages,
to belong to the narrator, for he is the only narrating 'I'
encountered so far. However, the speaker this time turns out
to be a garrulous old man, Mr Madden, who is sitting opposite the couple in a slow train. This stage of the journey is
clearly back in Hell; when Mr Madden disembarks, he calls
to them: 'Not alighting? said the old man. You're quite right,
only the damned alight here' (p. 40). A little digging will
disclose what area of the *Inferno* this interlude entails. Mr
Madden's long monologue about 'springing from the loins of
a parish priest' (p. 39) and verbally knocking into people
('Then up I'd get, covered with blood and my rags in ribbons,
and at 'em again,' p. 39) recalls the Fourth Circle of the
Inferno where damned souls, including a disproportionate
number of tonsured clerics, wheel in a great circle and collide
repeatedly with each other. In a passage whose end we
quoted earlier, The Unnamable associates Mercier and Camier
with the same Circle: 'Two shapes then, oblong like man,
entered into collision before me. They fell and I saw them
no more. I naturally thought of the pseudo-couple Mercier-
Camier' (*Unnamable,* p. 297). The Fourth Circle is connected
with Mercier and Camier, not from their point of view, but
from that of the narrator who invents their pratfalls. We see
now the reason both for Mr Madden's confusing entry into
the chapter and his invocation of the Fourth Circle: he is the
taking a journey but, unlike theirs, his is purely verbal. No
other character in the book, aside from Mr Conaire whom
we shall meet in a moment, delivers long monologues, for
such utterances are the dubious privilege of the narrator
alone. The particular Hell to which he belongs is different
from but just as insufferable as that which his creatures
inhabit. Hence, Mercier responds with amazement to his
suggestion that all three of them alight together: 'This puts a
fresh complexion on it, said Mercier' (p. 39). A change of
Hell might be interesting.

They finally get off one stop after Mr Madden and proceed

to Mr Gall's, alias Mr Gast, inn. Their difficult reception there recalls the defiant refusal of the devils to let Dante and Virgil past the gate of Dis. Once admitted, Mercier and Camier go upstairs, and during their absence another wayfarer, Mr Conaire, enters. If we attend to clues, it becomes obvious that he is a double of Mr Madden and hence another reflection of the narrator. Both Madden and Conaire are extremely talkative, carry walking sticks, and take a profound interest in the couple. The episodes involving each are termed 'interlude' in the chapter summary, the only ones so designated in the entire novel. Finally, Mr Conaire refers to the 'other hell calling me back' (p. 53); we can determine which part by considering his bald head, for the tonsured clerics of Mr Madden's Fourth Circle are also bald. The clinching proof that Mr Conaire, like Mr Madden, is an image of the narrator appears in a series of hints near the close of the chapter culminating, if we untangle the Dantean references, with Mr Conaire and the couple exchanging roles. First, Mr Conaire shrieks at the horrors of childbirth and the pudenda of adult women. This recalls Dante balking at the passage through fire on the Seventh Terrace of Purgatory (Canto XXVII) where lust is purged. At the end of his outburst, Mr Conaire sees his auditors 'smiling at him as at a child' (p. 54), exactly how Virgil regards the reluctant Dante, shying at the flames: '[He] smiled as one does at a child that is won with an apple.' Immediately after his painful purgation, Dante falls asleep. This is imitated in the novel where, directly following his little agony, Mr Conaire is informed that Mercier and Camier have fallen asleep. That the couple exchange roles with Mr Conaire should come as no surprise when we consider him as an image of the narrator for, as we have already seen, the narrator admits at the outset that their story is simply a means of preserving his subjectivity.[4]

The opening of Chapter IV mingles this Canto with the next. The barren field in which Mercier and Camier find themselves is yet another version of the Earthly Paradise, the setting of that next Canto (XVIII). The goat prancing along the hedgerow recalls the one to which Dante compares himself after passing through the flames. The narrator draws out the parallel, for it soon becomes obvious that he is comparing the goat both to himself and the couple; all of them move in circles: 'Would it continue thus all round the field? Or weary first?' (p. 56). Dante's sudden sensation of lightness after casting off the burden of sin is recalled in Camier's remark, following his disposal of an envelope of miscellaneous junk: 'So, he said, I feel lighter now' (p. 57). Camier is trying, as he says a little later, to disencumber himself of 'life in short' (p. 66), but this is something that the Beckettian Purgatory never quite manages. The futility of their intentions is underscored near the end of the chapter when Camier decides to abandon their precious raincoat. Such a gesture, instead of completing the purgation, only lands them right back in hell. Mercier says, 'I should have liked to launch it' (p. 65), and worries that, if they simply leave the garment on the ground, 'some verminous brute' (p. 66) will seize it. The words introduce a detailed inter- polation from Cantos XVI and XVII of the *Inferno*. The launching recalls Dante's throwing his belt into the infernal pit to signal the winged monster, Geyron, on whose back he and Virgil fly to the Eighth Circle or Malebolge. Camier's advice, 'lente, lente, and circumspection, with deviations to right and left and sudden reversals of course' (p. 67) follows Dante's description of the flight to the point of actually quoting two words from the Italian text (XVII, 115). Mercier's remark, '. . . if I look up I'll fall down' (p. 67), simulates Dante's dizziness. The chapter ends, as does Dante's flight, with the reaching of a different part of hell: 'Cheer up, said Camier, we are coming to the station of the damned, I can see the steeple' (p. 67).

As soon as the couple enter the town (Chapter V), they go to Helen's where the 'two-fold light of lamp and leaden day' (p. 71) that illumines their troilistic amusements points back to Dante's amazement in Canto I at the brilliance of Paradise: '. . . and of a sudden it seemed there was added day to day, as if He that is able and had decked the sky with a second sun.' When they leave at noon the next day, Camier remarks on 'the pretty rainbow', a feeble copy of the Beatific Vision that fills the last Canto of the *Paradiso* where Dante beholds the three circles of coloured light, the first two 'reflected by the other as rainbow by rainbow. . . .' The chapter ends with the couple again trudging off, and this time their journey will take them right through Purgatory with no digressions. Soon after leaving Helen's, they see an old man, reminding us of Cato at the base of the mountain of Purgatory. Then follows a series of significant details: the 'fog' (p. 78) that wraps Mercier derives from the spiritual 'fog' which Cato directs Virgil to wash from Dante's face before commencing the ascent. The narrator plays then with the word 'shadows', echoing the third Canto where Dante, not realising that only his body, still alive, casts a shadow in Purgatory, marvels at Virgil's lack of one. Finally, the strange image of Mercier looking at his feet 'as through shifting seaweed' makes sense when related to the swaying ocean reeds with which Virgil is instructed to clothe Dante in Canto I. Here, in each case, the chapter neutralises the tremendous energy these three details contain in the *Purgatorio*.

Chapter VI continues the movement through Purgatory by shifting to Camier waiting alone in a pub for Mercier whose sudden entrance alarms everyone. The narrator can only note the reaction; he cannot explain it. Yet, his extended comparison of the clientele to a flock of sheep 'startled by some dark threat' recalls Dante's description in Canto III of the troop of souls' frightened response to his shadow: 'As the sheep come forth from the fold by one and two and three and the rest stand timid. . . .' The narrator is stressing the link between Mercier and Dante by making the otherwise 'not easily affected' (p. 81) pub clientele partake of the souls' unease. The couple then leave the pub and their aimless steps take them faster and faster through Purgatory. Their dialogue leaves a trail of hints. First Mercier: 'By the ingle, said Mercier, snug and warm, they drowse away. Books fall from hands, heads on chests, flames die down, embers expire, dream steals from its lair and towards its prey. But the watcher is on the watch, they wake and go to bed . . .' (p. 86). Here we rush through a number of Cantos. The cosy 'ingle' points to the shoulder of rock in Canto IV upon which Belacqua, the man of sloth, sits. (We shall have much more to say about him later.) The creeping dream and alert watcher derive from Canto VIII where at night, snakes symbolising the sinful dreams before which the sleeping soul is still vulnerable, weave down to the Valley of the Princes in Ante-purgatory, and are driven away by two guardian angels.

The brutal encounter with the constable at the end of the chapter brings the couple for a second time to the Seventh Terrace, for their Purgatory is cyclic and futile. Mercier's question about the location of a whorehouse and his defense of 'venery' (p. 92) identify the theme of lust proper to the Seventh Terrace while Camier's 'scream of pain' recalls Dante's torment in the flames. Finally, Mercier's cryptic remark which puzzles Camier, 'the flowers are in the vase and the flock back in the fold,' (p. 94) compresses two passages from the *Purgatorio* that immediately follow the fire. The flowers come from Dante's dream of Leah (Canto XXVII) 'going through a meadow gathering flowers and singing. . . .' The flock, coming from the same Canto, we have already met in Chapter IV. It revives Dante's comparison of himself to a goat in a flock and Virgil and Statius to his shepherds: '. . . as the herdsman who lodges in the open passes the night beside his quiet flock. . . .' Mercier and Camier may triumph over the policeman, but the circular Purgatory in which they revolve will bring them back to the same flames by the end of the next chapter, and yet again in the final chapter.

Chapter VII takes Mercier and Camier on another run through Purgatory. The chapter begins with a 'descriptive passage' (p. 98) whose mention of altitude, sea, mountain road, and a small valley for sleeping, echoes the plain of Antepurgatory and the ascent beyond. Sure enough, at the close of the passage Mercier points to a wooden cross near the road, recalling the figured pavement of the First Terrace (Canto XII) that commemorates the painful deaths of the proud. The narrator's identification of the grave as that of a nationalist is one of Beckett's little jabs against his native Ireland. Mercier's admission, 'I don't think I can go much further' (p. 101), repeats the similar one Dante utters several times in the *Purgatorio*. The sudden approach of darkness, making everything 'blurred and fuzzy, as if you were going blind before your very eyes' (p. 101), duplicates the dense smoke that renders Dante temporarily 'blind' on the Third Terrace where anger is purged (Canto XVI). Mercier's offer to

take Camier's hand repeats Virgil's order to Dante: 'See that
thou art not cut off from me.' The night the couple pass in
some ruins derives from the Fourth Terrace where sloth is
atoned for (Canto XVIII) and which Virgil and Dante enter
near midnight. The Dantean purgation of sloth by its contrary, continuous movement, appears in the narrator's desire
to close his story at this point ('Here would be the place to
make an end,' p. 103) but he is unable to do so: 'But there is
still day, day after day, afterlife all life long, the dust of all
that is dead and buried rising, eddying, settling, burying
again' (p. 103). The cycle that drives him on makes him
propel the couple out of their shelter before dawn to resume
the journey, and so continue through Purgatory. Camier's
wave to Mercier ('But even to the dead a man may wave,'
p. 106), duplicates Virgil's salute to Statius on the Fifth
Terrace (Canto XXI), while the giant tree at the crossroads
derives from the one similarly placed in the next Canto.
Camier's hesitation and flight down one of the forks 'as into
a burning house' (p. 107) repeats once again the wall of fire
in Canto XXVII.

In Chapter VIII, the couple's encounter with Watt, hero of
Beckett's preceding novel, shunts them back several Cantos.
Camier's failure to recognise him recalls Dante's inability to
recognise Forese Donati on the Sixth Terrace (Canto XXII).
Their talk of Camier's saintly mother revives the praise
Forese heaps upon his widow, Nella. The couple and Watt
walk toward the sunset into a pub, just as Dante, Virgil, and
Statius in Canto XXV walk toward the setting sun to enter
the Seventh Terrace. Watt's mention of 'the utilities I was
stuck with at birth' (p. 113) echoes Statius' account of
conception and the creation of the soul in the same Canto.
Watt's agonised outburst, 'Bugger life!' (p. 114) and his
subsequent torpor ('Watt seemed asleep', p. 117) re-enact
a fourth and last time Dante's passage through fire. Despair
of life is the sin from which neither Watt nor the couple can
even be cleansed. Mercier's jest, 'Blessed be the dead that die'
(p. 115), mocks the admiring benediction Guido Guinicelli
confers upon Dante just before the latter enters the fire:
'Blessed art thou . . . who, to die better, takest freight of
experience from our bounds!' In Mercier's world there is

no experience but the same experience of vacancy repeated. Finally, Camier's cryptic utterance, 'the goat' (p. 117), points back again to Canto XXVII and Dante's simile after passing through the flames.

The book ends with Mercier and Camier sitting on a bench at dusk by a river, trying to spot flowers in the distance. The rather disappointing results contrast sharply with Dante's vision of the river of light and the multifoliate rose (*Paradiso*, XXX). Camier's parting gesture of 'pouring over' (p. 122) the river recalls Dante letting his 'eyelids drink' of the celestial river in this Canto. Mercier's concluding vision of darkness ('Alone he watched the sky go out, dark deepen to its full,' p. 122) brings us to a brutal inversion of the Beatific Vision at the end of the *Paradiso* and Dante's hymn to 'Light Eternal'. Such is the 'apparent consummation'[5] Beckett's Purgatory allows.

The advent of Watt together with Mercier's recollection of Murphy ('I knew a poor man named Murphy,' p. 111) make it clear that Dante's world is not the only one against which the journey of Mercier and Camier is projected. There is also Beckett's and of this the book contains much evidence. The pub owner, Mr Gall, whose name is quietly changed to Mr Gast, seems a suspiciously close relation to Mr Gall, the piano tuner, in *Watt*. Mr Graves also makes an appearance in both novels. The old man that Mercier spies 'carrying under his arm what looked like a board folded in two' (p. 76) recalls not only Cato, as we suggested, but the narrator of 'The End', a story written about the same time as *Mercier and Camier*: 'I had perfected my board. It now consisted of two boards hinged together, which enabled me, when my work was done, to fold it and carry it under my arm' (p. 157).[6] The narrator who accompanies Mercier and Camier is the same one who propels Murphy, Watt, and all the rest on their way. Just before meeting Watt, Mercier voices his intimation of the narrator's presence: 'Like the presence of a third party, said Mercier. Enveloping us. I have felt it from the start' (p. 100). This journey and all the other ones are so many attempts to forge the narrator's subjectivity through a plurality of personae.

At this point the worlds of Dante and Beckett intersect,

and the narrator resembles Belacqua.[7] Before entering
Purgatory proper, Belacqua must spend a second lifetime
in Antepurgatory dreaming over his first lifetime wasted
slothfully on earth. The Beckettian narrator, on the other
hand, with no hope of eventual bliss, must pass an interminable present dreaming of a past that was never his, reliving
through the couple and other characters a subjectivity that
he never had. As we have already seen from his first sentence,
the narrator has no self beyond the characters he invents. He
attempts through Mercier and Camier not only to gain his
subjectivity, but at the same time to express the futility of
his search for it. Otherwise the self he gains would not be his.
In different words, the narrator does not want any old self;
he wants just enough to let him utter his need for one, since
that need defines who he is. Caught in the endless cycle of
trying to express his own lack of self, his efforts can have no
genuine conclusion. This repetition is the very essence of
sloth, the Deadly Sin of Belacqua — reviewing the same
tedium again and again, without the energy to seek something new and fresh, something with a purpose. When E. M.
Cioran says that the weariness of Beckett's heroes is not of
this earth, he puts his finger on an important truth: this is
the fatigue of a being forever denied the hope of ceasing or
changing into something more definite.[8]

By sending the couple on their meaningless journey, the
narrator gives them just enough subjectivity to know what
they are missing: 'Looking back on it, said Camier, we heard
ourselves speaking of everything but ourselves' (p. 119). The
murmurs noted in the last sentence of the novel, while
Mercier sits alone in the dark, are the clearest expression of
what the narrator has been approaching all along. They enter
most of Beckett's works and intrude, for example, when
Molloy is stranded between remaining himself or becoming
one of his characters, A or C: 'Then the murmurs begin again'
(*Molloy*, p. 11). Heard by a subject who never realises that he
is their author, the murmurs are a Beckettian convention
signifying the inability of that subject to be himself. They are
the sound of his own endless dissolution, and for that there
is no purgation. The elaborate and repetitious journey of
Mercier and Camier is simply an alternative expression of this

experience of interminable dissolution where the notions of beginning and end or definite self and world no longer apply. In the next chapter, we shall see how Beckett expands this emerging experience of Nothing into a powerful enunciation of the human species in our own era.

5

Molloy, Malone Dies, The Unnamable: Beckettian Man and the Voice of Species

Beckett's Trilogy was written during a three-year period of intense creativity (1947—1949) often referred to as 'the siege in the room'. Here we enter the heartland of Beckett's prose fiction. In the first four novels, the narrator edges us toward his own experience, a whirling zone with neither self nor ordered sequence. In the Trilogy, fully aware of paradox, he begins to tell us what that unintelligible experience signifies. But before receiving his explanation, we must know a little more about the speaker.

Not too far into the Trilogy, Moran, after a strenuous analysis of the behaviour of bees, makes an observation that tugs slyly at the reader: 'And I said, with rapture, here is something I can study all my life, and never understand' (p. 169). The remark does more than discourage impetuous interpretations; it points out a basic extravagance in the text. Regardless of his name, the speaker in any of the novels never hesitates to undercut or undermine the statements that a moment ago he carefully assembled. If he so little respects his laborious explanations, why does he pronounce them? If, as seems equally true, he cannot avoid talking, why does he disown the stories so produced? We take a first step toward the answers by realising that, behind the various disguises, there is but one speaker in the three novels,[1] and no one is happier to stress this than he: 'This time, then once more I think, then perhaps a last time, then I think it'll be over, with that world too' (p. 8). At the end, he invokes what has preceded: '. . . then he says I, as if I were he, or in another, let us be just, then he says Murphy, or Molloy, I forget, as if I were Malone, but their day is done' (p. 403).

This is a strange literary creature, a narrator who tells

54

stories about his desire to narrate no more, a desire which cannot be satisfied before he knows who is telling them. Unfortunately, the problem of his identity seems insoluble; he can remember nothing but fragments of other stories told still earlier. The Trilogy constitutes a rather spectacular effort to exploit the very cause of his predicament by transforming the narrator into the stories he tells. To accomplish such a task he stations, at definite intervals, personae who relay the narration until it finally returns to its source. Helpful and disposable, personae provide masks and material; for, necessarily tied to particular situations as any of Browning's or Eliot's monologues will show, they already have something to talk about. Narration under such circumstances places a tremendous burden on the stories; they are responsible for the eventual liberation of their narrator. In order that the three novels may not collapse under the strain, each is sustained by some structural underpinning derived from an established literary form. In *Molloy,* it is the epic and the memoire. *Malone Dies* rests upon the death-bed confession, while *The Unnamable* deploys several, but stresses the philosophical discourse. Without the support of recognisable genres, the novels would be little more than the results of a strange narrative compulsion to 'blacken a few more pages. . .' (p. 68). Held by these literary forms, the reader steers safely through the stories as Ulysses past the Sirens, hearing the many voices, but never rushing madly toward them.

Yet the narrator does not care about readers; he just wants to finish. Every story, he knows, must have a beginning, middle, and end. Thus each novel in the Trilogy, aside from its own movement toward conclusion, embodies one of these three divisions. All of *Molloy* is an attempt to find a beginning, but the seeking is successively diverted onto different tracks by different seekers. Nothing moves successfully in a straight line; neither the personae nor their narration can avoid circular movement and inevitable return to the point of departure. When Molloy says, '. . . it was a bad beginning . . .' (p. 29) he speaks not primarily of a particular event, but of a story ill broached, forever wandering from its course. Molloy never gets beyond his uneasiness about the beginning of his story: 'Here's my beginning. Here it is' (p. 8) — indeed, by recounting the search for his mother, the one responsible for his own origin, he tells a story about beginning. Molloy travels, then hears 'a voice telling me not to fret, that help was coming' (p. 91). And so it does. Within a few lines, the narration is out of his hands and into Moran's. What does this mean? Molloy's search for a beginning has gone on unsuccessfully for so long that a replacement is sent in to make a fresh start. There is, of course, a regress here, a second beginning looking for the first. The true beginning will never be found, for that involves the origin of the Trilogy narrator himself, and as we shall see, this is precisely what cannot be known.

Like Molloy, Moran is a persona fashioned, in so far as he must tell a story ('It told me to write the report,' p. 176) in the image of his creator, the Trilogy narrator. Moran's 'mission', as he calls it, is to find Molloy and await further instructions. He leaves no doubt that in fulfilling this assignment he will be acting not so much in the role of professional spy or 'agent' as in that of designated narrator:

> Stories, stories. I have not been able to tell them. I shall not be able to tell this one.
> I could not determine therefore how I was to deal with Molloy, once I had found him (p. 137).

Moran is here clearly charged with the duty to continue the story of Molloy. This he pursues with such unwavering attention that not only is the story extended but so is its subject; Molloy lives on in Moran: 'He had only to rise up within me for me to be filled with panting' (p. 113). His mission accomplished, Moran ends, but not without remembering the preoccupation with beginnings. The closing disclaimer, 'It was not midnight. It was not raining,' returns us to the start of his story.

Similarly, *Malone Dies* seeks to establish a middle. The very title suggests a state intermediate between two others, and Malone emphasises this in his repeated images of birth and death: 'I am being given, if I may venture the expression, birth into death, such is my impression' (p. 283). Stuck between two terms, he is powerless to extricate himself and the longer he continues the more evident this appears. To while away his death-watch, Malone plans four stories, 'each one on a different theme' (p. 181), echoing the cycles of Chaucer and Boccaccio. Malone is so unable to manage his narration that he must frequently encourage himself: 'We are getting on' (p. 193), 'a last effort' (often used), 'try and go on' (p. 227). The Trilogy narrator, in creating Malone as persona, has put him in a very difficult situation; for death is simply not an act that can be narrated: a man cannot know his last words. Consequently, Malone must stall, clinging to the middle, desperately trying to make the end of his story coincide with his demise.

From one point of view, this takes *A Thousand and One Nights* to its logical terminus. Whereas Scheherazade tells stories to prolong her life in a world outside them, Malone drones on to end his life within one. His voracious appetite for material even includes reflections on his own interruptions: 'I fear that I must have fallen asleep again. I have just written, I fear I must have fallen, etc.' (p. 208). Under this kind of pressure, Malone grasps at anything to maintain his verbal momentum without caring much about sequence. The whole notion of plot device as something used to move the narrator on with his story has dwindled to Malone's beloved stick which no longer propels the owner literally or narratively, but merely brings possessions before him to be recorded when all else fails.

Such impoverishment should not surprise us; the symptoms appear in *Molloy*. There we find vestiges of the old narrative concern for linear continuity in the various means of locomotion available to Moran: autocycle, train, motorcoach, and bicycle. He ends on crutches. Plot has already been reduced to the bare necessity to go forward in any way possible. Indeed, the bicycles on which he and Molloy lavish such attention are not plot devices in the sense of moving the story to the next event. They simply afford an opportunity to narrate: 'I would gladly describe it, I would gladly write four thousand words on it alone' (p. 155).

Finally, *The Unnamable* toils to reach the end as desperately as the first two novels strive to establish a beginning and middle. Tumbled into his narration before he can devise a named persona, the true narrator (The Unnamable) trundles out stock phrases of introduction or exordium: 'These few general remarks to begin with' and 'In the beginning'. Already his master scheme has failed, for with the death of Malone, ending is no longer a matter of stories but of their narrator, and this throws up again the question of his identity. Narrators are governed by the same laws as their stories; neither can end without a clear beginning. The narrator must know his own origin before he can depart, and thus his dilemma remains unsolved: 'I hope this preamble will soon come to an end and the statement begin that will dispose of me. Unfortunately, I am afraid, as always, of going on' (p. 302). The notions of beginning and end recur four times in the first sentence of this passage, and 'going on' becomes an endless cycle. If he is ignorant of his own history and cannot remember a time when he was not making it up, then the stratagem of the Trilogy is foredoomed.[2] How can he transform himself into a story that ends if there was never a genuine separation between himself and his narration in the first place?

We have already discussed in the Introduction how The Unnamable is a *pure narrator,* defined only by his relation to words and silence. Now we are in a position to see how Beckett is able to transform this formal narrative predicament into a vivid experience of confusion and strain. Narration is literally The Unnamable's life. Each word pushes his existence a little farther, and so comes out with great effort and intensity. There is nothing to fall back on, not even his previous words, for there is no clear end to which they lead and no certainty from which they spring. The difficulty of ending grows more apparent. Words are all the narrator has, but, having them, he loses himself; for which ones belong to him alone without dragging in the beliefs and associations of strangers? Each word, borrowed from the community of men, compromises the isolation of which he tries to speak and, by translating the purity of an experience uniquely his own into the coarser terms of a public language, subverts the very purpose of narration. Far from overcoming this impasse, the narrator is everywhere limited and embittered by it: 'Is there a single word of mine in all I say?' (p. 347). Even worse, what can he do when their number shrinks? We see this clearly near the end when The Unnamable's phrases progressively shorten, until they are merely clipped formulae, gathered in groups by repeated words. Only with great effort can he sufficiently jostle the phrases so that his thought can procede. He records them sliding away: '... they took away nature, there was never anyone, anyone but me...' (p. 395). Terrifyingly, the passage that follows contains no words for concrete objects.

The flight of words denies the narrator freedom. In the opening page of the Trilogy, before he has adequately introduced himself, the narrator refers to some unidentified visitors as 'they'. This pronoun appears throughout the work, and where the antecedent is unclear it is always 'words'. They are the ones who dictate the story, the narrator little more than a scribe:

> What I'd like now is to speak of the things that are left, say my goodbyes, finish dying. They don't want that. Yes, there is more than one, apparently. But it's always the same one that comes. You'll do that later he says. Good (p. 7).

We realise that the visitor is the word 'good', noncommital and cheery, ready to help the narrator through any impasse. He uses it a few lines further on: 'I've forgotten how to spell too, and half the words. That doesn't matter apparently. Good. He's a queer one the one who comes to see me.' Here the connection between the word and the visitor is explicit. Malone, lying in a hospital bed, has a similar visitor, except that this time it is the word, 'goodness': 'I don't know why she is good to me. Yes, let us call it goodness, without quibbling. For her it is certainly goodness' (p. 185). The irony in both cases is bitter: a sick narrator tended by a member of the tribe that plagues him.

His problem with 'the silence' is part of this narrative disease. He is down to the bare bones of narration: words (a voice) breaking the silence. In health, silence is the best friend of any narrator. It can spare disproportionate detail, fuel suspense (as in detective novels), and cast a shadow of appealing mystery (as with the question of Marlowe's own sentiments in *Heart of Darkness*). The Unnamable realises that silence has many implications: 'for it is all very fine to keep silence,

but one must also consider the kind of silence one keeps'
(p. 309). Moreover, silence is the material and final cause of
narration; it is that from which a story is shaped and that to
which it tends. A story may be told only if a little area of our
verbal world is cleared of words and made fresh for a narrator's
contribution; it grows up and falls back in the blankness;
otherwise, we would never hear. This narrator, however, cannot enter the silence for, never having properly begun, he
never quite left it.[3] So he remains, murmuring in the Purgatory between ending a story falsely begun and beginning the
silence only partially ended.

With no definite boundaries to protect him, the narrator
must constantly heap up words to keep himself distinct from
his story, otherwise he cannot join it at the end and gain
silence. Molloy's celebrated story of A and C will illustrate.
Listen to him labouring to keep boundaries visible:

> A and C I never saw again. But perhaps I shall see them
> again. But shall I be able to recognize them? And am I sure
> I never saw them again? An instant of silence, as when the
> conductor taps on his stand, raises his arms, before the un-
> answerable clamour (p. 15).

In the passage we see the uncontrollable fission that everywhere undermines the narrator. His simplest statement splin-
ters into a series of regressive questions and hypotheses, each
leading farther from the object (in this case A and C) and
growing more preoccupied with the subject. In *The Unnamable,* the fission actually enters the narrator, but he has
only himself to blame. The plan of having Malone enter a
story about his own narration and so end both the story and
persona in the same breath backfires; for after Malone disappears, the narrator behind him still remains. When the
narrator tries the same strategy on himself, the results are dis-
astrous. Unlike Malone, the narrator cannot make his story a
mirror of himself, for he is already nothing but his own reflection. That is, his only existence is a questioning of that
existence, a reflection of that existence in myriad hypotheses: 'Where now? Who now? When now? Unquestioning. I,
say I. Unbelieving. Questions, hypotheses, call them that' (p.
291). In other words, he is a series of hypotheses about him-

self, and cannot reach back from them to himself speaking for, apart from them, he is mere confusion. In fusing with his questions, he loses the 'I' uttering them, and can refer to it only as an anonymous voice: 'Ah if only this voice could stop, this meaningless voice which prevents you from being nothing. . .' (p. 370). But this is just the beginning of his problem. If he cannot claim the voice, then neither can he find himself in its hypotheses, for their very presence rests on the absence of the self they seek to construct: 'it's not I' (p. 409) or 'perhaps it's I' (p. 413). Perhaps if he holds up a second mirror to reflect the way he is already reflected in hypotheses, the narrator will at last have an image of himself that he can speak of and so regain his voice. Accordingly, he conceives Worm who, as a purely narrative object, has no existence beyond the hypotheses that form him. Worm has no private or independent subjectivity. He is nothing but others' conception of him or, more precisely, he is only what words (others) express him to be: 'Feeling nothing, knowing nothing, he exists nevertheless, but not for himself, for others, others conceive him and say, Worm is, since we conceive him . . .' (p. 346). The ploy must fail. Since the narrator is already a reflection of his own need to seek an 'I', reflecting himself as Worm in a second mirror only multiplies images of the same need. It does not cure that need. The voice is farther away than ever.

Nevertheless, the narrator is still related to the voice in one respect. It is his in so far as it shares the prime narrative duty to bring matters to a just and proper conclusion: 'Perhaps I've said the thing that had to be said, that gives me the right to be done with speech, done with listening, done with hearing, without my knowing it' (p. 394). The moral weight of the voice, implied above by the word 'right' is underscored by Molloy who refers to 'imperatives' while Moran clarifies its narrative significance: 'For it is within me and exhorts me to continue to the end the faithful servant I have always been, of a cause that is not mine. . .' (p. 132). His mission is to finish a story begun by another narrator (Molloy) at the instigation of a third (the Trilogy narrator). In this moral scheme, words are the means of executing narrative obligation and silence is the end. When the words themselves become a pure expression of the duty to go forward, the narrator, saying at last what is his need and no one else's, retains his voice in time to go silent. The Unnamable's closing phrases are worth quoting in this light: '. . . you must go on, I can't go on, I'll go on.'

A voice of such candour must be narrating more than its own persistence. Indeed, the Trilogy contains much evidence that, beyond himself, the narrator speaks for mankind, but in a very original way. The process of stripping away narrative conventions has also peeled back social ones. Moran is the first to make this clear. He loses everything that once confirmed his personal identity: his clothes, his physical agility, his son, his huge bunch of keys and the property they locked. Yet, as these drop away he grows increasingly conscious of knowing himself more vividly. Musing on this one day, he has a vision recalling that of Narcissus by the pond. He sees a face not his but unquestionably human:

> And then I saw a little globe swaying up slowly from the depths, through the quiet water, smooth at first, and scarcely paler than its escorting ripples, then little by little a face, with holes for the eyes and mouth and other wounds, and nothing to show if it was a man's face or a woman's face, a young face or an old face. . . (p. 149).

This is Beckettian Man, with nothing of his own save resemblance to his species. His voice is no longer the private wail of one man in pain, but that of humanity, the human species. The Trilogy abounds with such references. Molloy reminds us 'I am human' (p. 78); Malone indicates Macmann's 'link with his species' (p. 241); while The Unnamable states 'it's human, a lobster couldn't do it' (p. 372).

After seeing his own face as the face of species, Moran is visited by a 'dim man, dim of face and dim of body' (p. 150). Moran's description continues for several lines, yet deals only with the overall 'harmony and concord' of 'his various parts'. We realise that the man, having no definite personal features, is recognisable only in so far as he belongs to the species and is, therefore, another embodiment of Beckettian Man. Later, Moran, in a transport he cannot remember, brutally murders the intruder. To understand this act of violence we must recognise that it is the culmination of a tightly related series of events. The day before, after studying his reflection in a stream, Moran had received another visitor, an older man with a 'massive' stick and 'a huge shock of dirty snow-white hair' (p. 146) who asked for bread and departed. Evidence points to Malone, for early in his own narration Malone mentions his 'big shaggy head' (p. 184) and 'vaguely' recalls wandering in a forest before waking up in the bed he now occupies. Since each visitor enters shortly after Moran muses on his own image, each reflects him from a different point of view. The first man attracts him; the second repels. Moran is drawn to the narrator (Malone) in himself, but is horrified by the species that pursues him. The dim man, in fact, seems to shadow narrators with great tenacity, for he announces that he seeks the first visitor. By killing him, Moran attempts to preserve his own identity as an individual. Instead, he immediately loses one of the few remaining trappings of individuality — his keys — and is more vulnerable to the tedium of nothing in particular to do which, as we shall soon see, so haunts the species. Moran has not destroyed the intruder; he has become him. He cannot drive out species any more than The Unnamable can help 'getting humanized' (p. 360). The narrator must always speak as Beckettian Man with the vestigial voice of his species.

Malone's stories demonstrate this clearly. Their characters have experiences to be sure, yet these concern not personal problems but the unmitigated suffering of human existence. That is the denominator to which all individuals are reduced. The young Saposcat, unwittingly adumbrating the torpor of *The Lost Ones,* almost lapses into a world where all are 'vanquished in a mad world' (p. 193) and individuality cannot endure. Mrs Lambert, exhausted by routine, loses even the ability to complain; her laments become a 'pantomime' (p. 202) of Woman Grieving: 'The bosom — no, what matters is the head and then the hands it calls to its help before all else, that clasp, wring, then sadly resume their labour. . . .' Macmann, despite attempts to lose humanity ('And a good half of his existence must have been spent in a motionlessness akin to that of stone,' p. 243) cannot escape the pains of 'the struggle for life' which always 'prod him in the arse' (p. 243).

Emphatically, it is survival, not individuality, that counts.

Beckettian Man is not an Everyman. Whereas the latter is an individual capable of reflecting on himself, his own particular sins and salvation, Beckettian Man can consider only those attributes or specific differences that mark man off from other species. Accordingly, all judgments are strikingly general, the personal details vague. Molloy barely recalls his mother as an individual; she is more an indispensible principle. Malone lingers over a childhood, but not his own. After Malone's demise, the narrator, unable to die and make an end, will 'resurrect' (p. 393) in the next novel. Perhaps nothing is more piteous in the entire Trilogy than the loss of this most personal act, the one where, if its approach is not sudden, a man can take stock of his entire past and, on the basis of that evaluation, consign himself to eternity. Species, of course, must continue as long as one representative survives, as those haunting last phrases of the text declare. Without death, even sin, due no longer to the Fall of the first man but to the origin and existence of the species, bears no relation to an individual error: 'I was given a pensum, at birth perhaps, as a punishment for having been born. . .' (p. 310).

To consider man from the standpoint of species rather than individuality is to overthrow every traditional source of his greatness. The result is not his abjection or humiliation, but simply his futility. A species can accomplish nothing, not even its own termination. It is merely the formal statement of qualities which any individual must have in order actually to be a member of that species and not another. Merging man with his species imprisons him in a changeless universe of abstraction where his noble properties still work but with nothing to work on. Consequently, they fall back on themselves in blind obedience to their functions.

The most reknowned of human qualities is rationality. In the Aristotelian definition, man is a *rational* animal; that is the specific difference setting him apart within the wider genus, animal. Once the supreme centre of experience in the Humanist tradition, reason, in Beckettian Man, is reduced to a restless inquiry into its own nature. Throughout the Trilogy, the 'rational animal' makes many appearances as the faculty of reason itself, now an untameable brute tormenting instead of enlightening.[4] To Moran, the beast is Molloy, prowling inside him 'like a bear' (p. 113), seeking the reason for existence; for Malone it is no less formidable, clawing always for an explanation: 'While within me the wild beast of earnestness padded up and down, roaring, ravening, rending' (p. 194). With The Unnamable, reason is a caged beast with nothing to seek but the cause of its seeking which, of course, is itself, and all the while afraid of its own movement. The following passage describing this condition, suggests that the cause lies in the endless succession of generations that sustains species:

> . . . I seek, like a caged beast born of caged beasts born of caged beasts born of caged beasts born in a cage and dead in a cage, born and then dead, born in a cage and then dead in a cage, in a word like a beast, in one of their words, like such a beast, and that I seek, like such a beast, with my little strength, such a beast, with nothing of its species left but fear and fury, no, the fury is past, nothing but fear, nothing of all its due but fear centupled, fear of its shadow. . . (p. 387).

The 'fury' mentioned in the quotation indicates the second human faculty — will. For to Beckettian Man fury is merely frustrated will: 'Because of the will I suppose, which the least opposition seems to lash into a fury' (p. 139). Will is the uncompelled tending toward a goal or end, and The Unnamable is correct in linking it closely to reason.[5] For in Humanist tradition, reason is responsible for determining goals and holding them before the will. With Beckettian Man, reason, knowing only its own ignorance,[6] can offer the will no assistance, and the will, deprived of guidance, retains the characteristic of movement but with no direction. Malone speaks of his 'throes' (p. 179), spontaneous twitchings of the will that literally have no reason. Will is reduced to a mere tending or straining triggered by obstacles rather than goals. Moran puts this starkly:

> The more things resist me the more rabid I get. With time, and nothing but my teeth and nails, I would rage up from the bowels of the earth to its crust, knowing full well I

had nothing to gain. And when I had no more teeth, no more nails, I would dig through the rock with my bones (p. 156).

The dependence of will upon reason in Humanist doctrine is reversible: reason itself is powerless unless urged by the will to pursue its inquiry. When we speak of rationality, we speak also of the will. This relationship forms the basis of man's moral nature, where will and reason co-operate in both idea and act. The 'rational animal' in Beckettian Man displays this conjunction in rude form; fear and fury are the vestiges of reason and will.[7] The seeking which ordinarily expands toward the good end here goes on endlessly. We now have another way of understanding the narrator's 'imperatives' to continue. They are all that remain of the moral sense or 'earnestness' as Malone has called it. This is an indelible attribute of the species, but one that, without individuals, can have no consummation; for morality involves choices and choices require acts. Species has no choice and only individuals can act. The moral impotence of species supports a striking paradox in the Trilogy — the ceaseless movement in that which is immobile. The very core of Humanist morality concerns the achievement of *arete, dignitas,* or beatitude (depending on whether we regard the Greek, Roman, or Christian strands) through the training of reason and will on their proper ends. Beckettian Man, himself a species, cannot change, yet recalls the striving of individuals who do. The Unnamable's subtle placement of the initial comma in the following passage shows how wide yawns and gulf between species and individual. He, of course, speaks as species; an individual would eliminate the comma: 'No, one can spend one's life thus, unable to live, unable to bring to life, and die in vain, having done nothing, been nothing' (p. 358).

Freedom has no meaning in a universe without choices, where acts can only hopelessly reiterate their own moral impotence, but this is exactly what all the narrator's little stories do. Through the Trilogy he understands this more and more clearly. Moran near the end of his story raises a question and answer: 'Does this mean I am freer now than I was? I do not know' (p. 176). Malone, more experienced than his predecessor, tries to fabricate a pseudo-freedom within these impossible limits: 'There is a choice of images' (p. 196). All his narrative efforts, however, ultimately express the same moral bondage, the same inability truly to act, truly to set upon a path. This The Unnamable admits: 'I haven't stirred, that's all I know, no, I know something else, it's not I, I always forget that, I resume, you must resume, never stirred from here, never stopped telling stories, to myself, hardly hearing them. . . (p. 412).

After reason, will, and morality, Beckettian Man has a fourth characteristic — habit. This again derives from Humanist thought and is called *habitus* 'in the jargon of the schools' (p. 51). As such it designates the special capacity of reason and will to respond to exercise and develop stable dispositions or states of readiness. The philosopher's intellect, for example, acquires the *habitus* for speculative thought. In Beckettian Man, we find a remnant of this malleability in the building of habit; yet, where in the earlier tradition *habitus* is the result of conscious application, Beckettian habit is the passive acceptance of any restriction. Moran, developing a progressive pain in his knee, forgets that it was once healthy: 'That is to say it was perhaps a little worse, without my being in a condition to realize it, for the simple reason that this leg was becoming a habit, mercifully' (p. 147). There is, in fact, only one thing that cannot be absorbed by habit, and that is boredom. Beckettian Man, being a species, has no notion of fulfillment, only the tedious repetition of individuals. Species cannot improve; the most it can hope for is extinction. Hence, any activity, even contemplation of God, is just a tiresome series of identical moments: 'Might not the beatific vision become a source of boredom, in the long run?' (p. 167).

Beckett's use of a narrator to express his vision of mankind is strategic and fruitful. Insulated from author and from intruding conventions, he is the perfect mouthpiece for a species isolated in its own uniqueness. Beckett has created a purely literary figure whose existence is qualified only by his relation to his own words and, estranged from himself in uttering them, he is completely alone. Repeating stories about his personae, the narrator imitates the species sustained by generations of individuals. We are not given a metaphysical discussion, but rather a fiction of species thinking itself, cut off from the hierarchy of being to which it formerly belonged.

The narrator, through Moran, compares himself to Sisyphus forever going over the same route, bound to a task that has no conclusion. This too is species suffering numberless instantiations, never getting closer to completion. Yet, Beckettian Man, duped by isolation into confusing his singular species with individuality, thinks that 'each journey is his first', or at least that it will be his last, and occupies a worse position than Sisyphus who has no expectations: 'Whereas to see yourself doing the same thing endlessly over and over again fills you with satisfaction' (p. 133). In the same passage, Moran, mentioning Sisyphus' obligation 'to rejoice, as the fashion is now', makes a backhand reference to Camus' *The Myth of Sisyphus.* The entire problem of absurdity that Camus there raises is dismissed in the Trilogy. Absurdity arises where man's demands for rational explanations go unheard by a deaf and purposeless universe. This is not the case with Beckettian Man whose world is highly ordered by the inevitable circularity of his movements. Whatever the words or inventions, he always returns to the species enveloping him. Absurdity involves a polarity between two terms: dumb universe and questioning man. Beckettian Man, in contrast, knows no polarity; there is no term beside himself.

Despite a superficial resemblance, solipsism has no place here, for it presupposes a world unknown in the Trilogy, a a world where a discrete subject, finding no means of proving that the objects given in experience exist independently of that experience, concludes that nothing but itself is real.[8] Now, the narrator can never be accused of this error; for he remains ignorant of any subject ('I shall not say I again . . . it's too farcial,' [p. 353]) and, even were he to gain one, the words would always prevent him from expressing it. Moreover, he cannot find the world that any good solipsist so readily envelops: '. . . let us go on as if I were the only one in the world, whereas I'm the only one absent from it. . .' (p. 401). Where solipsism affirms nothing but the experiencing subject, the Trilogy engages in a search for that subject, i.e. the narrator. The most ingenious attempt is launched by Malone through whose death the narrator hopes to pare away any particle of experience not coincident with narration, and to confront himself at last. The experiment is successful up to a point — there is no experience left but narration; that narration, however, must endlessly declare the impossibility of finding its narrator: I'll speak of me when I speak no more. . .' (p. 392). The situation could not be otherwise for a narrator has always to occupy one time and place while telling another. Denied the conventional boundaries of narrated past and narrating present, the Trilogy narrator often uses 'here' and 'there' or 'elsewhere' to refer to irreducible absence at the core of narration — speaking of being there when one is here: '. . . there I am the absentee again. . .' (p. 413). Molloy does just this in his opening sentences already quoted: 'It's I who live there now. I don't know how I got there.' The adverb 'there' places him in the story; his 'here' is something completely different and inaccessible. In this context, 'here' means not a place or an object at all, but the act of narrating or, in other words, the *actual* speaking. In a desperate effort to find himself 'here', The Unnamable attempts to reverse the relation by speaking of a voice seeking him, approaching his 'here': 'a voice like this, who can check it, it tries everything, it's blind, it seeks me blindly, in the dark. . .' (p. 410). In so doing, he hopes to empty his own narrating act of all content so that eventually all of him will be narrated and 'there' in the voice. The ruse is futile. If successful, the voice would still be speaking of its inability to 'say me' (p. 414), and the regress would be infinite.

The best parallel to this kind of absence appears not in the waking world of solipsism, but in the world of dreams where the dreamer only regains himself upon waking. The Unnamable acknowledges the connection:

> . . . perhaps it's a dream, all a dream, that would surprise me, I'll wake, in the silence, and never sleep again, it will be I, or dream, dream again, dream of a silence. . . (p. 414).

It is as if the narrator has fallen into a dream about his identity, a dream that always moves on so that, unless he keeps up by asking questions, he will fall behind hopelessly confused. Molloy suggests: '. . . ask yourself questions . . . to keep you free from losing the thread of the dream' (p. 49).

The hope is to go on until the end when the narrator will wake up and be himself: '. . . no matter who I am, no matter where I am' (p. 302).

The analogy from dreams emphasises The Unnamable's powerlessness to analyse his experience, to divide truth from falsehood or past from present. Nevertheless, his notion of dream is fundamentally different from the one we as individuals entertain. Where we always know that waking will restore a familiar self, The Unnamable, knowing nothing but his present, can make no clear distinction between waking and sleeping. This undifferentiated experience is precisely that of species thinking itself, with no respite, no variation, no means of possessing anything personal, not even the chance of remembering a dream after waking. All that remains of man's glorious enterprise of self-knowledge is the reflex of introspection gone on so long that its individual subject is lost. As with the narrator's dream, there can be no issue; for the notion of species is itself the result of man's introspection into his own nature, not *qua* individual, but *qua* man. Born of introspection, it seeks by introspection to find itself.[9] Again, the regress is infinite, as the narrator's fabrication of personae to satisfy the introspective habit shows. Ideally, the act, directed from a self, returns to its source and contains its object. Pure introspection has no movement, as the centre of a circle knows simultaneously all the circumference, Beckettian Man, however, is stranded on the circumference, hopelessly seeking the beginning, doomed to revolve as long as there are generations.

In other words, Beckett is saying that the very foundation of personal identity has been eaten away, and it is easy to see why. According to Humanism, the most basic question any individual can ask in an effort to gain self-knowledge is not 'Who am I?' but 'What is man?' for to know oneself one must first know what it means to be a man. The object of self-knowledge is not something internal and hopelessly shut up but an intelligible essence — *humanitas* — shared by all men and through which, if they choose to accept the spiritual demands it implies, they are truly themselves. Yet, *humanitas* only has meaning when the human species occupies its proper rung on the vast Humanist ladder of Being. That is, *humanitas* belongs to each man in so far as he is a member of the species yet species in turn has no meaning by itself but only in a much wider universe of classification.

Beckett is conveying a truth here that no one before him has had the strength or courage to pursue. His vision of man is painful but somehow must be communicated. I am re- minded of a wonderful remark made by Maynard Mack in the course of a discussion of Shakespeare: 'Doubtless one of the anguishes of being a great artist is that you cannot tell people what they and you and your common institutions are really like — when viewed absolutely — without being dismissed as insane.'[10] Indeed, the Beckettian narrator, who is Beckett's surrogate, often bravely raises the question of his own in- sanity only just as bravely to deny it. But the people who cannot accept his vision and who abuse him for it are them- selves roundly abused by the narrator: 'And in the evening I turned to the lights of Bally, I watched them shine brighter and brighter, then all go out together, or nearly all, foul little flickering lights of terrified men' (p. 162). The real folly is to remain comforted by the little fires we all build to keep away the void that is in and around us.

Beckett's vision may be called post-metaphysical. It re- sponds to the need for a universal ordering of being but knows that there is none. For with Beckett all the old assump- tions of man and universe are so deliberately relinquished that human experience is left to formulate vainly its own re- sulting complexity. Those hapless formulations constitute Beckett's voice of species.

6

Texts for Nothing: Farewell to Being

To my mind, *Texts for Nothing* has always been the most difficult and elusive of Beckett's works. Who or what is the voice that talks so steadily and with such strange peace through thirteen monologues? As we saw in the Introduction, this voice, like The Unnamable, is a pure narrator stranded between the two poles of narration, words and silence. Yet, why is the Text narrator so much more resigned to futility and ignorance than his predecessor? His utterance moves with the quiet cadence of a chant, very different from the increasingly frantic mutterings of The Unnamable. It will be worthwhile to press the comparison between these two voices. Both seek their own subjectivity and grapple with the problem of continuing. But there are some important differences. The Unnamable is driven by the ambition to reach a narrative end. For this reason, he constructs the first two books of the Trilogy, hoping with the conclusion of *Malone Dies* to finish forever. When that attempt fails, he still seeks to end within the boundaries of a story, and so spins his yarns about Mahood, Worm, and a handful of other variations of his plight. The Text narrator, on the other hand, goes beyond telling stories. Strictly speaking, as we shall see, he is not trying to do anything but merely go on giving up. Where The Unnamable's impulse is literally fictional, wanting to move inside his narration, that of the Text narrator is what might be called, 'theoretical', pursuing a series of questions and answers about his inability to enter any story.

In fact, each of the Texts introduces a question and ends with a provisional conclusion which does not so much answer the query as remove the possibility of its being properly asked. Ultimately, the narrator's questions concern his

inability to pose them. It will be helpful to sketch these:
Text 1: Why did I start the narration? Answer: I'm doing the
same thing over and over again. Text 2: Where can I go with
my story? Answer: There is no more hope of going anywhere. Text 3: 'What matter who's speaking. . . ?' (p. 85).
Answer: No one has spoken. Text 4: Who is narrating, claim-
ing to be me? Answer: As soon as I speak, the voice is no
longer mine. Text 5: Why do I want the story to be mine?
Answer: I am haunted by phantoms through whom I speak.
Text 6: 'How are the intervals filled between these apparitions?' (p. 101). Answer: If I could enter an interval and
know that I was in one, then perhaps I could at last begin
a story that would end. Text 7: Have I looked everywhere
to find me? Answer: I am not to be found where life is,
i.e. where time actually moves ahead. Text 8: Were things
always so? Answer: I have always been asking that question.
Text 9: Why don't I say, 'There's a way out there'? (p. 117).
Answer: If I could say it, I would pass out of here. Text 10:
Can mere utterance make sense? Answer: All I'm trying to
do is go on. Text 11: What am I saying? Answer: '. . . that is
all I can have had to say this evening' (p. 131). Text 12: Will
the words succeed in slipping me into him they describe?
Answer: Here are nothing but lifeless words. Text 13: How
do I get out of here? Answer: I am nowhere.

   Something very strange is going on here. Far from telling a
story, all the narrator can express is ignorance about his own
utterance — a radical ignorance that has not appeared before
in literature. The use of questions may initially deceive us
into believing that the narrator has only to go on asking them
in order at last to gain the knowledge he seeks. But look
more closely at those questions. What emerges through them
is not knowledge but an admission of the impossibility of
ever attaining it. For example, 'What am I saying?' yields
'. . . that is all I can have had to say, this evening'. The
answers are not answers but the denial that any exist. In fact,
the question-answer or catechetical format is merely a device
to indicate that narration has entered a realm where the
impulse to ascertain truth and falsehood still remains but
where every attempt to do so is doomed to fail.

   Beckett's aesthetic of failure underpins this paradoxical

work. In 1949, a year before writing *Texts for Nothing*,[1] Beckett wrote *Three Dialogues with Georges Duthuit* and presented his view of the function and dilemma of the artist in this century. He argued, as noted in the Introduction, that in every work of art and in every age the artist is trying, at bottom, to express or illumine one or both of the two poles of human experience — self and world or subject and object. When the contemporary artist strives to follow this tradition, however, he runs into difficulty; for all the naiveté, dogma and/or faith enabling artists in the past at least to assume that self and world were manageable and intelligible concepts have evaporated. The contemporary artist is left with the task of grappling with concepts he cannot define and cannot use. If courageous and faithful to his vocation as an artist, he will not turn away from this impasse, but rather will make it the centre of his work. Instead of englightening or giving definite form to the two poles of human experience, the artists can now only express his failure to do so. He must 'admit that to be an artist is to fail, as no other dare fail, that failure is his world and the shrink from it desertion, art and craft, good housekeeping, living'.[2]

In another essay, 'Peintres de l'empêchement',[3] Beckett discusses two ways of confronting this predicament. The artist can choose to express that which obscures the notion of world and object or that which obscures the notion of self and subject. The painter taking the first path depicts not the object but everything which prevents him from grasping it. He thus tries to express the 'indifference'[4] of the object, its inaccessibility. The painter taking the second path represents not himself or his modes of perceiving (as, for example, Cézanne does in his studies of Mt Ste Victoire) but everything that impedes him from such knowledge. Thus, he conveys the absence of any definite self or subject: '. . . an isolated being, enclosed and shut up forever in itself, without a trace, without air, Cyclopean, glimpsed midst lightning flashes and spectral shades of black' (p. 157).[5] These two alternatives are problems of expression which, in Beckett's opinion, have been solved — one each and with admirable frugality — by two painters, the van Velde brothers. Yet, in *Texts for Nothing*, Beckett attempts what no one else has dared: the expression of both alternatives. In fact, many of the phrases used by the Text narrator duplicate those I have just quoted. Speaking of the absent objective world, he too recalls the 'indifference' (p. 80) of objects. The greatest number of echoes occurs when referring to the inability to find a subject: 'an isolated being, enclosed and shut up forever in itself' becomes 'if there was a way out' (p. 119); 'without a trace' becomes 'a trace, it wants to leave a trace' (p. 137); 'without air' becomes 'there is no air here' (pp. 137–138); 'glimpsed midst lightning flashes' becomes 'a gleam of light' (p. 140); 'spectral shades of black' becomes 'the extinction of this black nothing and its impossible shades' (p. 139).

Through the Text narrator, Beckett fulfills his aesthetic of failure. The Text narrator is so unable to relate himself to either the subjective or objective pole that his utterance is no more than a repeated admission of impotence: 'I'll have gone on giving up, having had nothing, not being there' (p. 125). But his powerlessness goes much father than this; it constitutes his very being. Even the term 'narrator' with its implication of a stable character is misleading, for what we have here is an endlessly unrealised act of expression, impossibly suspended between its inaccessible subject and unattainable consummation. The act of speech or expression, instead of enabling an agent or subject to realise his end, itself generates two further acts — listening and then speaking about that listening: 'I say it as I hear it' (p. 97). What we have, then, is a futile act of expression alienated from its own agent — 'Who says this saying it's me,' (p. 91) — and forever denied any fulfillment or end — 'Give up, but it's all given up, it's nothing new,' (p. 123). The same problem arises when the narrator, as this vain act of expression, tries to link agent and end by telling a story of himself. The 'I' in the narration remains unrelated to the 'he' narrating him, for the act of expression recedes from its object or end just as from its subject or agent: '. . . I wait for me afar for my story to begin, to end, and again this voice cannot be mine' (p. 94). He is caught between trying to find himself in a story and trying in that story to find himself narrating it.

Considered as an act of expression unrelated to any agent

or end, the Text narrator contravenes the classical logic which holds that, since an act *is* the tending of an agent toward his end, no act can exist without its two necessary terms. How, then, can we refer to an act of expression under these conditions? Or, alternatively, how does the narrator manage anything more than mere utterance, mere babbling in a void? The question is so important that the narrator does not hesitate to raise it: '. . . there is utterance, somewhere someone is uttering. Inanities, agreed, but is that enough, is that enough, to make sense?' (p. 123). The narrator hopes to solve this problem of expression persisting in the absence of both agent and end by making that expression its own agent. This means that the act of expression must express itself. Since, in this case, words are the act of expression, it is words that must be expressed: '. . . with what words shall I name my unnamable words?' (p. 105). Even if this were possible, it would involve an infinite regress; the words that named his words would in turn need to be named, and so on.

The narrator's incapacity to act is absolute: 'here nothing will happen' (p. 90), and constitutes no less than a metaphysical impotence. The narrator more than once insinuates the connection between his futility and Being:

How long have I been here, what a question, I've often wondered. And often I could answer, an hour, a month, a year, a century, depending on what I meant by here, and me, and being. . . (p. 76).

Or again:

. . . deep in this place which is not one, which is merely a moment for the time being eternal, which is called here, and in this being which is called me and is not one. . . (p. 131).

These allusions suggest that to understand the full implications of the narrator's impotence and his experience of Nothing we must treat it on the most fundamental level of all — the level of Being. But we must proceed very cautiously.

Being is not an easy word to define, and once defined it is often more difficult to understand. The concept may perhaps be better explained if we consider first the impulses leading to its formulation. In classical philosophy — and this is one source of Beckett's own approach – the concept of Being results from a passionate attempt to place human knowledge and the world it encounters on an absolutely sure foundation. To do this, the mind must turn from a consideration of mere particulars or phenomena which constantly change to a contemplation of universal or abiding forms which operate everywhere and to which everything is related. The mind must then follow these forms back to their source and thus reach the First Principle or Absolute toward whose perfection everything tends. This attempt to discover an Absolute from which everything may be derived but which itself is completely independent and fulfilled is called metaphysics or the science of Being. We cannot hope to follow classical metaphysics without realising that for these philosophers the intellect is capable not just of conception but of genuine intuition, direct contact with real forms. This does not necessarily entail a distrust of the senses, for in certain schools (e.g. those of Aristotle and Aquinas) the mind can grasp forms only by first abstracting them from sensory presentations. It does mean, however, that the intellect, unlike the senses, can remain in the presence of its objects, unconfused by local circumstances such as light and dark. The intellect intuits, therefore, an eternal world of reality and not a mere appearance dependent upon a finite perspective. A careful distinction must be made here. Modern schools of philosophy such as phenomenology, following in Kant's wake, want to extract from the welter of human experience the structural principles on which it rests, without worrying too much about the objects toward which that experience is directed. On the other hand, classical metaphysics, taking the fact of experience for granted, seeks the true structure of the universe available to but in no way limited by experience. In this case, the intellect works as a kind of metaphysical X-ray, penetrating beneath the flux of superficial appearances to see things at last as they truly are — related to an Absolute in whose perfection they participate to the extent they themselves express an abiding principle or form. We are to think of Being, then, as a vast hierarchy or system, every part of which strives toward the formal perfection of the Absolute at its summit. Nothing, in contrast, denotes that which is completely without relation to a universal form and is hence unintelligible to reason.

This description of Being is incomplete, for it has only treated the topic from a structural point of view, as an object for the intellect. Right from Aristotle, however, there is a desire to grasp Being from the inside, as it is to itself. From this internal point of view, Being is not a static ontological arrangement but a dynamic simultaneity of acts whereby each link in the chain of Being strives to express a form or essence. Through the act of being proper to it, each ascending link enjoys the potency or potential to realise a more universal form than the one preceding and, by fulfilling that potential, earns a higher measure of *act*uality. For a seed, that act is to realise the form of species latent in it by becoming a plant; for man it is to expand his knowledge, to learn the order of universal forms. For God, the Absolute, or Pure Being, which alone possesses full actuality, that act is, 'according to Aristotle, who knew everything' (p. 114), to think on its own thinking; for that thought, at once grasping all forms in a unity of intellection, is the supreme act whose universality is progressively reflected but never equalled by all the other acts in the hierarchy of Being.

If we listen again to the voice of the Text narrator, the full significance of his words will be clear. His futile struggle to define his universe in terms of one supreme act (the act of narration) descends directly from the metaphysical impulse of Humanism stretching down from Aristotle. The human need for metaphysical certainties and explanations persists, but the means to fulfill that need have gone. Through his narrator, then, Beckett gives expression to the predicament of human experience in our age — desperately seeking the solace and justification offered by the great systems of Being but no longer able to receive them. The plea of ignorance which the narrator repeatedly makes is ultimately metaphysical, an ignorance of Being, and derives from Book IX of the *Metaphysics* where Aristotle states that knowledge of Being is an all or nothing proposition; you either have it or you don't: 'About the things, then, which are essences and actualities, it is not possible to be in error, but only to know them or not to know them.'[6] Where there is metaphysical knowledge, there is, *ipso facto,* truth; where there is no such knowledge, the terms for truth and falsehood simply do not apply. It is in this light (or darkness) that we can best understand the Text narrator's oscillation between affirmation and denial. 'Yes' and 'no' alternate so frequently that no distinction between truth and falsehood can obtain. This is the very essence of ignorance as Aristotle describes it.

Nevertheless, there is one big difference between the ignorance Aristotle mentions and that of the Text narrator. For Aristotle, metaphysical ignorance arises from a simple lack of appropriate training. For the Text narrator, in contrast, ignorance arises because there is no longer anything metaphysical to know. The great universe of Being has been abandoned but nothing has been constructed in its place. Where once the defining function of the human species was the use of reason to uncover and articulate the universe of Being, reason can now do no more than ponder its inability to find anything. Deprived of the older tradition, reason can now only contemplate a void where once was a universe teeming with universal forms.[7]

We find here a profound pathos and nostalgia. Being, as we have found, is the only way of relating the existence of individuals and, beyond them, their species to an eternal structure by which they are justified and fulfilled. In bidding farewell to Being, Beckett mourns the last hope of finding any permanent meaning or explanation to a human predicament that begins from nothing and ends in death. This the Text narrator admits in his final words:

> And were there one day to be here, where there are no days, which is no place, born of the impossible voice the unmakable being, and a gleam of light, still all would be silent and empty and dark, as now, as soon now, when all will be ended, all said, it says, it murmurs (p. 140).

The utterance is certainly one of the most ambiguous in any literature, and underscores clearly the absolute impotence of Beckettian being. At first glance, the passage seems no more than an elaborate sentence fragment. What is the redeeming wish implied and implored by the subjunctive mood in the initial clause? In fact, there is a choice of three, each one undercut by a contradiction. The first two are easy to point out. The narrator, in his futility, is asking that either (1) 'there' be here or that (2) 'one day' be 'here', where there are no more days'. The third redeeming wish is more subtle and involves the infinitive 'to be': 'And were there one day *to be* [i.e. a true act of being] here ... born of the impossible voice the unmakable being. ...' The narrator duly subverts this last alternative by invoking his version of the ancient law, *ex nihilo nihil fit*. No 'to be' can come from 'unmakable being'. Hence, the triple wish occasioning the subjunctive mood dies before it can be answered. Being will always confront its own impossibility. In the closing words, the narrator, as always, cannot claim his own voice, his own 'I' or agency: '... it says, it murmurs'. The absolute act, the perfect self-knowledge, that crowns Being in the shining tradition of Humanism shrinks with Beckett to the eternal search for an agent and a world in which he can be.

It is here that I disagree with those critics who find that Beckett is writing about writing, that his art primarily concerns its own difficult act of creation, and hence that all references to elusive voices point ultimately to the author's struggle to pin down his own literary inspiration.[8] When the narrator observes that another voice speaks through him, he is not so much indicating the author as symbolising through this predicament the general impoverishment of Being. The narrator's awareness of his own lack of being points to the need for being that fills us all.

We touch here the final paradox of *Texts for Nothing*. For Beckett, Being is not so much a fixed and intelligible structure intended to outlast the ages as a profound expression of the human need to comprehend experience in each new age. The need for Being is interesting only in so far as it points back to the Nothing it tries to overcome. Beckett's attitude is strikingly ambivalent on this point. From one angle, he seems to mourn the departure of Humanism; from another, he regards that departure as a liberation, for only in the absence of system can the human spirit seek fresh expression of its predicament, only in the absence of Being can the need for Being be aroused. And it is this need for Being that has inspired some of the noblest enterprises of the human species.

Beckett's fascination with this experience of dislocation and improvisation, when all the old guidelines are down, goes all the way back to his second publication — the study, *Proust*. There, Beckett develops his theory of Proustian being in a way that at once foreshadows his own notion of being and indicates how different that notion is from the one he reads in Proust.

Beckett finds that Proust's creatures are not stable selves inhabiting stable worlds. What is called self or world is simply a Habit, a means of building and perpetuating something familiar and of pushing out or ignoring what is strange. But let us hear Beckett's own words on the matter, since no one can put it more clearly than he:

> Life is habit. Or rather life is a succession of habits, since the individual is a succession of individuals; the world being a projection of the individual's consciousness (an objectivation of the individual's will, Schopenhauer would say), the pact must be continually renewed, the letter of safe conduct brought up to date. The creation of the world did not take place once and for all time, but takes place every day. Habit then is the generic term for the countless treaties concluded between the countless subjects that constitute the individual and their countless correlative objects. The periods of transition that separate consecutive adaptations . . . represent the perilous zones in the life of the individual, dangerous, precarious, painful, mysterious and fertile, when for a moment the boredom of living is replaced by the suffering of *being* [my italics].[9]

In the Proustian formula, to suffer — i.e. to struggle unprotected by habit, world, self, and other familiar constructs — is to be. To be is to attend with every faculty to one's predicament, one's present. To be is to be conscious of nothing familiar, to realise or affirm that all constructs are false and that without them we, as selves inhabiting worlds, are not.

Beckett's remarks on Proustian being, no matter how unsympathetic towards conventional notions of self, never dispense with the necessity of a personal centre undergoing the suffering. The fleeting moments of Proustian being are, as already quoted, 'the perilous zones in the life of the individual', and with this phrase a multitude of assumptions, untenable in the more severe climate of Beckett's own fiction, are invoked. For Beckett the extermination of self and the world that self projects is but a preliminary movement, leading ultimately to the dissolution of individuality and of the Humanist universe on which individuality is based. In other words, the seedy solipsism of Murphy and his private third zone is just the first step on the road to the metaphysical wilderness of The Unnamable and the Text narrator. Where Proustian being is of a liberated individual, Beckettian being refers, not to the experience of one finite centre suddenly denied the solace of Habit, but to the predicament of the species today, cast out from the metaphysical and theological haven which once comforted it. Beckett applies the personal abandonment he finds in Proust to the spiritual abandonment he finds in this century. In other words, Beckett is taking Proust to his logical conclusion. Where Proust reveals personal being by eliminating Habit, Beckett reveals the need for universal Being by eliminating all its habitual, Humanist expressions.

7

How It Is: An Allegory of Time and Personal Identity

How It Is, first published as *Comment C'est* in 1961, initiates a new direction in the evolution of Beckettian fiction. In the earliest narrations, Beckett approached the experience of Nothing by progressively pushing out and constricting all familiar and worldly contexts until finally arriving at the void from which the narrator speaks in both *The Unnamable* and *Texts for Nothing.* In *How It Is,* however, the narrator, through his persona, Bom, inhabits a very definite subterranean world, crawling 'right leg right arm push pull' across an endless expanse of mud. The change is not surprising. Beckett is exploring new ways to express the experience of Nothing, and so resorts to allegory.

The motive for the allegory in *How It Is* is clarified by a remark made much earlier in *Watt:* 'This fragility of the outer meaning [of experience] caused him to seek for another, for some meaning of what had passed, in the image of how it had passed' (p. 73). The meaning of 'what had passed' will be immediately clear only if the experience in question can be given a definite form. If, however, the experience is precisely an experience of Nothing, then meaning can emerge only through constructing 'an image of how it passed', only, that is, by building a structure whose definite form will, paradoxically, reflect the formlessness of the original experience and give it meaning. This structure is allegory. To succeed it must sustain, as Beckett suggests in his essay on Proust, a separate, 'literal, special, and concrete' (*Proust,* p. 79) reality which, vivid and arresting in its own right, can illumine some aspect of the experience it symbolises. Thus, the literal and concrete world of *How It Is* is an attempt to express some aspect of the formless experience behind it. That aspect is the

83

absence of time or, more loosely, the sense of succession in experience. Beckett is expressing the human need for a concept of time while showing that temporality is just another empty, structural hypothesis necessary to give human experience significance and meaning. As Fernand Saint-Martin writes at the end of his *Samuel Beckett et l'univers de la Fiction*, 'The very substratum of human existence is revealed [in Beckett's universe] as the experience of creating time.' He adds, 'This fundamental intuition makes the tragic grandeur of his *oeuvre* and makes Beckett one of the greatest writers of our century' (p. 265).

In one astonishingly simple movement, space becomes a symbol for the absence of time. The narrator has already declared this transformation in *Texts for Nothing:* '. . . time has turned into space and there will be no more time, till I get out of here' (p. 112). The recurrent phrase in *How It Is,* 'vast tracts of time', clearly shows — even while insisting that there is still plenty of time — how time has become space. Of course, to talk of space or vast tracts in *How It Is* is inevitably to talk of the mud that stretches everywhere; for in this allegory Beckett wants to make the absence of successive time as concrete as possible. As far as Bom, the narrator, can peer, there is mud. Scrabbling in an endless counterclockwise direction across it, moving fitfully 'ten yards, fifteen yards', Bom has no way of distinguishing where he is (the present) from where he has been (the past) or from where he is to go (the future). Since the mud has no boundaries and is not contained by anything, it has (according to Aristotelian logic) no place whatsoever. If Bom has no place (a position in space), then he has no position in time, no way of sorting out 'this immeasurable wallow'.[1] He is in a far worse position than Molloy who at least had access to distinct muck heaps, and would vary his circumstances by 'moving from one muck heap to another' (*Molloy,* p. 41).

Mud powerfully symbolises the endless experience of Nothing, an experience without the procession that time confers. Mud is a soggy substance composed of an indefinite number of particles none of which can be differentiated. The experience of Nothing, then, is a whole without discernible parts or phases that can be ordered in any definite succession.

The sack that Bom clutches while scrambling across the mud reinforces this notion. By suggesting the placental sack and the umbilical cord, it points back to the impossible beginning of this experience — impossible because beginnings are only in time and here there is none: 'the cord a burst sack I say it as I hear it murmur it to the mud old sack old cord you remain' (p. 46).

To show that the need for time in human experience derives from a more fundamental and unalterable chaos or meaninglessness, Beckett must also assail the notion of personal identity; for time and personal identity are mutually dependent. Hence, in *How It Is,* personal identity dissolves in paradoxes. Bom's dwindling sense of personal identity is underscored by his use of pronouns. Occasionally, he says 'we' when actually referring to 'I': 'Pim we're talking of Pim' or 'I was young I clung on to the species we're talking of the human' (p. 47). Bom uses 'we' when in danger of losing his train of thought, when the train is in danger of derailment. Paradoxically, the plural destroys the uniqueness and singularity necessary to personal identity.

The paradoxes ravaging his personal identity multiply. If Bom in his use of 'we' is not fully aware of being an individual, can he be aware of being a member (i.e. an individual member) of a species? And to turn the paradox on its head, can Bom cling so desperately to the species without losing his individuality? Bom, of course, clings, because to lose species is to lose individuality; for a particular (individual) requires a universal (species) in order to be logically intelligible *as a particular.* The thin membrane of personal identity rips under the tension of its two poles. Bom can remain an individual member of a species only if he knows other individual members of the same species. Otherwise, he becomes a species unto himself, a species with one member, as with the angels in Thomistic theology. But the difficulty remains, as Sir David Ross has suggested: 'Though a species may in fact have only one member, the nature of a species is to be capable of having more than one. How then is each of the [angels] distinguished from the thinkable though non-existent members of the same species?'[2] Bom recognises this: 'with someone to keep me company I would have been a different man more universal' (p. 67). Personal identity is threatened by isolation: 'hanging on by the fingernails to one's species' (p. 26).

The link between the breakdown of personal identity and the absence of time is perhaps most clearly evident in what happens to memory in *How It Is*. According to Locke, memory is the principle of individuality:

> . . . in this alone consists personal identity, i.e. the same-
> ness of rational being: and as far as this consciousness can
> be extended backwards to any past action or thought, so
> far reaches the identity of that person . . .[3]

Locke never considers the possibility that memory, as an 'extension backwards to any past action or thought' may be blurred if the 'extension backwards' rarely finds anything sharp and particular like a 'past action or thought', but rather encounters only mud — an indefinite sprawl of indistinguishable, endlessly repeated thoughts and actions. Memory, far from confirming Bom's identity, can only prove the unvarying identity of his experience. His experience — the proper object of memory — is too consistent (like mud) for any particular thing to be remembered. Bom eventually recognises that he cannot verify his memories, that he cannot distinguish between memory and fantasy: 'they are not memories no he has no memories . . . he can't affirm anything' (p. 97).

The plight of memory in *How It Is* shows how far we have fallen from the certainties of earlier eras. Bom's references to memory and 'the light' bear some relation to a defunct Augustine. As Etienne Gilson interprets the Church Father, 'to learn and to know intelligible truth is, therefore, to remember, in the present, the everlasting presence of divine light in us.'[4] An act of memory in the present reveals eternity (God). In *How It Is,* as we shall see, eternity is more problematic, and divine illumination becomes the private and uncertain operation of memory: 'ABOVE the light goes on little scenes in the mud or memories of scenes past. . .' (p. 98). Even the stratification of the universe into the place here, the place above (heaven), and the place below (hell), collapses inside Bom's mind and is lost in the vast tracts of horizontal mud. To rescue personal identity from complete dissolution, Bom tells the story of his torturer-victim relation with Pim. In tormenting Pim, Bom is trying to affirm his own identity but another paradox crops up here. Torture, as Sartre argues, proves to the torturer that 'man is an animal who must be led with a whip.' Further, it forces the torturer to know that he is 'bearing down upon himself as much as upon the victim'.[5] If personal identity emerges only in relation to other human beings, how can Bom preserve his own identity by treating Pim as an animal?

The relationship between Bom and Pim is never one between two human beings. As a torment or a lesson, it dispenses with Pim's humanity, and by hinting that both Bom and Pim see their relationship as that between frail man (Pim) and a deity (Bom), it expunges Bom's humanity.[6] By playing God, if only through the act of narrating Pim, Bom enjoys the ability to choose moments. He can, if not create something, at least modulate his own tedium. Yet, far from attaining divinity, he further dehumanises interpersonal relationships. For neither Pim nor Bom, neither man nor God, has any concern for the other — man in responding in order to minimise his discomfort, and God in teaching in order to forestall his boredom. The only thing agreed upon by both torturer and victim is the limitation of man: 'I am not going to kill myself demanding something beyond his powers that he stand on his head for example or on his feet or kneel most certainly not' (p. 64). The limitation is so pronounced that we cease talking of a man or a God at all.

If the relationship between Bom and Pim fails to secure their humanity, it also denies each his individuality. In the first place, tormentor and victim are reducible to what, in logic, is called an 'ordered pair'. Both terms are two-place predicates; that is, each implies the other, as with the terms, 'father' and 'son'. Beckett sees tormentor and victim as so closely related that they cannot exist as separate individuals:

what we were then each for himself and
for the other
glued together like a single body in the
dark the mud (p. 122)

Second, neither torturer nor victim, according to Beckett, is a complete term (father and son are complete terms). The torturer can torture only as long as his victim is present (whereas, once a son, always a son). When the victim escapes, the torturer changes to what Bom calls an 'abandoned'. The victim, after departing, is called a 'traveller'. The traveller crawls until he meets an abandoned whom he immediately torments. A cycle of rotating identities emerges:

> hard to conceive this last when instead of beginning as a traveller I begin as victim and instead of continuing as tormentor I continue as traveller and instead of ending abandoned
> Instead of ending abandoned I end as tormentor (p. 129).

The narrator treats this cycle both synchronically and diachronically. In the former, he enumerates, with characteristic, arithmetic precision, the respective positions of the one million individuals caught in the cycle. His readiness to treat people as numbers or geometric terms shows how little he regards experience as capable of individuation or retention: 'for number 814336 as we have seen by the time he reaches number 814337 has long since forgotten all he ever knew of number 814335 as completely as though he never had been' (p. 121).

Diachronically or historically, the cycle extends endlessly backward. From this point of view, Bom is part of an immemorial dynasty, all the sons of which have participated in the cycle. Bom's own voice blends with a much older, 'ancient' one, 'the voice of us all' (p. 139). However, this is only a ploy to give Bom a coherent past. As we shall note, he later admits that the only voice is his own.

The cycle collapses for another reason. Each of its four movements is governed by the notion of abandonment. The traveller is an abandoning victim; the torturer presses the victim through 'fear of being abandoned' (p. 66). Can we then talk of a cycle — a movement of time marked by recurrent phases? If abandonment determines all four phases of movement, if all are merely the same state seen from different points of view, then not much remains to distinguish one phase from another. Bom eventually admits that the figures of tormentor and victim cannot be differentiated: 'the two couples that in which I figure in the north as tormentor and that in which I figure in the south as victim compose the same spectacle exactly' (p. 131). The separate identities of Bom and Pim merge; they are identical: 'each one of us is at the same time Bom and Pim tormentor and tormented' (p. 140).

Individuality and personal identity are further undermined. Bom attempts to imagine a definite number of individuals, all identical, all repeating the futile effort to lie about their isolation by inventing the four-phase cycle. Yet, if all men are identical, they cannot be separated. Plurality becomes singularity; the human species has no individuals: 'but that in reality we are one and all from the unthinkable first to the no less unthinkable last glued together in a vast imbrication of flesh without breach or fissure' (p. 140). The simile, 'like a single body', that Bom used earlier now becomes fact.

But this statement, too, explodes. If neither personal identity nor individuality is possible, then far from involving all others in his plight, Bom cannot even talk about himself. In losing his identity, he loses his name (which seems to be a simple anagram for 'mob'). All he retains are his isolation and his voice talking of isolation: 'only me yes alone yes with my voice yes my murmur yes' (p. 140). He can say how it is and that it is his, but he cannot say who he is. He cannot be somebody if he knows nobody.

The entire report about Pim and of the four-phase cycle evolving from him represent an attempt to divide an absent time. The structure, 'how it was before, how it was with Pim, how it is after Pim', resembles the trinity of past, present, and future. Yet there never was a time with Pim that can be distinguished from any other time with Bom. With time absent, the identity of everything else is lost. Since nothing is distinct, and even the poles of void and plenum fuse, we cannot call this a world of illusion; for no separation between appearance and reality applies. We can, perhaps, call it a state of ignorance, where we can talk with certainty about nothing in particular, and can, conversely, talk incessantly about the sameness of everything in general. Bom endorses this interpretation:

and no again I'm sorry no one here knows himself it's the place without knowledge whence no doubt its peerlessness (p. 123).

The ambiguous phrase, 'no doubt', reveals a remarkable paradox in *How It Is*. Where there is no knowledge, there is no doubt. If I cannot know, then I know I cannot doubt. Again Augustine is overturned. His renowned proof of personal existence and identity — *si fallor, sum* (if I doubt, I am) — is impossible in the mud. The doubt that confirms Augustine's existence (the argument appears in Book XI of *The City of God*) cannot help Bom.

Still, Bom's ignorance and his attendant lack of doubt enable him to maintain an exquisite balance between despair and endurance. He knows, at least, that there is nothing in life to hope for. He knows, too, that he cannot doubt. With this remnant of knowledge, he persists and is aware of persisting: 'I am not dead to inexistence not irretrievably' (p. 69). Here are the two poles of his state: (1) patience to continue living, and (2) expectant desire to die. The final paradox awaits resolution. Bom (or the voice using that name) will pant through life until death arrives.

The paradox has another, more hideous solution. Bom's story is of a human soul who does not know that he *has* died. Just as he clings to a body that was never born ('old sack old cord'), so he gropes toward a death that has already happened: 'I SHALL DIE.' There are a number of hints that Bom may be a damned soul. First, the image of Bom crawling and feeding down there on the mud is not the representation of a living man of flesh and blood. Second, the frequent references to 'the life above', which we have already noted in a different context, intimate that the region below, in the mud, is hell. Third, Bom has just enough sense of God and of grace to be forever tormented by their absence. In a remarkable passage, he invokes an image of the Holy Ghost, embodied as a bird, dispensing 'saving' or efficacious grace. That the bird is an albatross and not the more emblematic dove emphasises the vague guilt and pang of loss from which Bom suffers:

on the muddy belly I saw one blessed day saving the grace

of Heraclitus the Obscure at the pitch of heaven's azure towering between its great black still spread wings the snowy body of I know not what frigate-bird the screaming albatross of the southern seas the history I knew my God the natural the good moments I had (p. 31).

The tremendous distance between 'muddy belly' and 'the pitch of heaven's azure' implies that Bom has fallen irrevocably.

What does this bizarre type of damnation signify? The answer lies in a comparison between Bom's damnation and the kind envisioned by the Christian theology whose echoes we have heard in *How It Is*. In that theology, the distribution of souls in the Afterlife was based on a very definite notion of personal identity. In the case of the wicked, for example, damnation was at once the consequence and final confirmation of their identities in life. Furthermore, the damned were utterly without time and therefore without hope; to be damned was to be beyond the solace of time. Now we can see the complex circularity of Bom's condition: his damnation, as suggested, is not to know that he has already been damned; he cannot know that he has been damned because that would involve knowing his identity; he cannot know his identity because he is damned (i.e. without time). In this allegory of Man, 'present formulation', human experience has no escape from the hopeless efforts to establish its own meaning.

An overwhelming sense of loss fills this voice of species that speaks through Bom, for time and personal identity are not all that he lacks. The words 'loss' and 'abandoned' recur throughout the novel. Beckettian Man has lost everything which once ennobled humanity; he is down in the mud trying in rage and despair to narrate a world which, however impoverished, reflects something of the old Humanist ideals: 'we have our being in justice' (p. 124), 'lying where abandoned penalty perhaps of their recent exertions but effect also of our justice' (p. 143), 'restore me to my dignity' (p. 26), 'there's a noble past' (p. 53), 'honour of the family' (p. 83), 'the wish for a little beauty' (p. 12). In short, the voice laments 'the little that's left of the little whereby man continues' (p. 26). The ideals of Humanism have led nowhere, and without them the experience of species is an empty cycle, a cycle which Beckett's fiction re-enacts in different ways. We cannot speak of time in this context, for time is not a series of recurrent moments. It is a succession, an ordered series, grounded in the assumption that experience leads somewhere, that each moment is a different moment, growing from the one preceding.

The narrator has always recognised that this kind of successive or endured time is not part of his experience. The Unnamable speaks of 'another instant of my old instant' (p. 400), and admits that he understands 'nothing about duration' (p. 407), nothing about the relation of one moment to its predecessor. *How It Is* represents a monumental effort to recapture time itself, not just the past. The easy confidence with which Proust explores time has long disappeared, and the narrator embarks upon a quest that Proust never dreamed of — a literal *recherche du temps perdu*. To this end, the narrator employs every tactic possible. Chief among them is the attempt to reclaim time as a genuine succession giving form and meaning to experience. The elaborate story of before, with, and after Pim, with its attempt to establish past, present, and future, constitutes an agonising failure to rise from the mud of lost time or no time and improvise true succession. Again and again when referring to narrated events, Bom says, 'natural order', trying by this means to reinforce the idea of unalterable sequence proper to time. His need to narrate a history or story is the need to order time, to have a time to order. When that ruse shatters, Bom advances another in order not to lose time altogether. If time is no longer divisible into discrete parts, perhaps it continues as an infinite series. Hence, the long hypothesis about the journey of tormentors and victims: '. . . so on infinitely' (p. 317).

Underneath these more comprehensive efforts to fabricate time is a far more modest and desperate one — the maintenance of the present. This, as the title suggests, is the fundamental concern of *How It Is*. If the narrator can give the illusion of a genuine present where the now changes moment by moment, perhaps he can get time going again for only in time can he hope eventually to end. Otherwise, experience is the same 'immeasurable wallow' (p. 141), the same 'black

night of boundless futurity' (p. 137). And so in vain he repeats words simulating the inexorable march of present time
into the future: 'ten seconds fifteen seconds'. From this
point of view, we can see that memory, so often invoked by
the narrator, is important not in the Proustian sense of revealing a past truth but in the Beckettian sense of guarantee-
ing a present which remembers. When, after a visitation of memory, Bom utters, 'good moments they were good moments', he
refers, not to the moments of the remembered past, but to
the moments of the recent present during which he did his
remembering. They were good moments because they were
distinct moments, filling the present with the illusion of time.
Even after these illusions dissolve, the narrator still has a last
means of manufacturing time, and that is the very act of
narration. The phrase, 'present formulation', appears repeatedly and applies to the narrator's choice of this story to
represent his predicament. He gains a kind of present by telling it.

Even the rhythm of Bom's monologue, the panting of ex-
haustion and monotony, is a heroic attempt to express the
present. Breath has always served Beckett as a symbol of
habit or taking life for granted. In *Proust* he says: 'Breathing
is habit. Life is habit' (p. 19). By *How It Is,* there are no
more habits, no more safe structures or systems. Breathing is
no longer automatic; not even the present can be taken for
granted. Elsewhere in Beckett's work (e.g. *Waiting for Godot*),
the act of waiting is sufficient to create time, to give the illusion that time is passing. But Bom is too far down the road to
Nothing for this act any longer to be available. He is, as he
says, 'Belacqua fallen over on his side tired of waiting' (p. 24).
And we must not make the mistake of thinking that, if Bom
has no time, at least he has eternity. The *totum simul* of eternity is reserved for God. Bom's attempt to claim it for himself is just another hypothesis to assure him of a present:
'vast tracts of time a few minutes on and off added up vast
stretch eternity same scale of magnitude' (p. 104). Time and
eternity, the one experienced as succession or duration, the
other as the wholeness of one encompassing moment, are
absolutely incommensurable; yet here Bom insists the contrary: 'same scale of magnitude'. His experience bears rela-

tion to neither time nor eternity, for his is the experience of Nothing.

8

Looking for *The Lost Ones*

Eliot in his celebrated essay, 'Tradition and the Individual Talent', points to the necessity of inclusive perspective in literature; awareness of what has gone before enriches the understanding of what follows, just as the significance of precedessors is completed or even formed by their followers. Certainly few living writers can match Beckett's sensitivity to a continuous and historical culture, but he goes further. In a magnificent reflexive act, his work embraces its own ancestors, and creates a fully articulated tradition. The more vigorously he advances his own *corpus,* the more strenuously must he eliminate others. Beckett's thrust is not linear, not progressive but circular, revolving around its point of origin, explicating with each orbit what was implicit in the beginning. He is the first to insist upon this. One of his critical pieces on the van Velde brothers written in 1948 emphasises the obligation to repeat the same conviction over and over again:

> Fortunately, it's not a question of saying what has not yet been said but of saying again, as often as possible and in the most reduced space, what has already been said.[1]

The Lost Ones demonstrates, as clearly as any of Beckett's longer efforts in prose fiction, how much each successive work depends on what has preceded. This is not simply a matter of treating familiar themes. Beyond these, the text reaches back to earlier works for both the details of the story and its narrative approach. As we shall see, the fundamental problem with which the narrator is grappling concerns his awareness of having always dealt with the same predicament. The best way for us to understand his difficulty is first to consider his story.

The text introduces us to a severely geometric world: the interior of a cylinder where a tribe of naked bodies pursues a barren existence. Crowded into a small space, each body has just enough room to stand. Since each is moved by the need to search 'for its lost one'[2] and indeed seems animated by nothing more than this necessity, some order must prevail in the cylinder for motion to be possible. Accordingly, the floor is divided into three different zones. The central one, by far the largest, is called the arena. There bodies circulate clockwise as best they can until the need to search drives them to the second zone, a narrow band where people march in single file counterclockwise around the arena they circumscribe. From this zone, provided his entry is matched by a corresponding exit, a body may gain access to the third, 'a belt about one metre wide' (p. 27) bounded on its outer edge by the cylinder wall. This last area contains fifteen ladders of irregular length used to convey climbers to the niches or tunnels: 'These are cavities sunk in that part of the wall which lies above an imaginary line running midway between floor and ceiling and features therefore of its upper half alone' (p. 11). Also in this zone remain 'a certain number of sedentary searchers sitting or standing against the wall' (p. 28). Only their eyes still seek relentlessly what they will never find. The zone also harbours four of the five 'vanquished' — bodies that, although alive, have lost all will to seek and crouch motionless with heads bowed. Near each ladder are 'queues' of bodies waiting their turn to ascend. Once at the head of the line, each has the right to carry his ladder along the narrow zone until reaching an appealing niche.

Conditions in the cylinder are as forbidding as its design. Both temperature and light are in flux, the former oscillating between twenty-five and five degrees centigrade, the latter alternating rapidly between two fixed limits of brightness with almost stroboscopic effect. At rare intervals, both temperature and light suddenly stop changing: 'Then all go dead still. It is perhaps the end of all. A few seconds and all begins again' (p. 8). At such moments, the bodies instantly freeze in place, holding their poses until the tumult resumes. A 'stridulence' or 'murmur' accompanies this flux and, except during the periodic arrests, is the only universally audible sound in the cylinder.

Such rigorous construction admits neither freedom nor purpose. The opening sentences indicate the circularity of the quest: 'Abode where lost bodies roam each searching for its lost one. Vast enough for search to be in vain. Narrow enough for flight to be in vain.' Lost Ones searching for their lost ones, intent on nothing but the hunt, reacting only when the unchecked momentum of one disturbs the orderly progress of all — this defines a state of collective absence where each, looking for what concerns him alone, helps build a prison that care for none. In this world of restless movement, waiting becomes the fundamental ordering principle. Ordinarily, waiting, by preceding action, permits everyone in turn to exercise freedom of choice. It is one way of reconciling individual liberty with social control. Here, however, action itself is determined by the need to seek and waiting, holding as its end the resumption of seeking, only confirms necessity.

The Lost Ones are hemmed in as much by necessity as by the cylinder walls, but how can we determine what this necessity is? To every guess we make about the object or end of their seeking, there is always a negation. The text makes it clear that their seeking has no goal but its own continuation. The search is neither for self ('None looks within himself where none can be,' p. 30) nor for another ('Whatever it is they are searching for it is not that,' p. 36). Seeking, moreover, has nothing to do with eyesight. The eye functions not as an organ but as a symbol either of this need to search or, in the case of the vanquished, of release from such compulsion. We are told that, moved by no impulse other than habit, the vanquished are liable occasionally to resume the motions of seeking. At such times, they wander 'unseeing' and are 'indistinguishable to the eye of flesh' (p. 31) from those still seeking. Obviously the eye is not what helps the remaining seekers in their search, for they are readily able to distinguish the errant vanquished from their ranks and step aside: 'These recognize them and make way' (p. 31). Similarly, the blindness of the vanquished is not a physical handicap, but the result or expression of a complete absence or oblivion where nothing whatsoever, neither self nor object, enters the mind.

A world so severely formulated draws attention to its maker, and a comparison between my earlier summary and the actual text will show that *The Lost Ones* concerns the limitations of narration far more than the torment of bodies in a cylinder. The story becomes a symbol or means of representing the movement of the narrator behind it, and only by remembering this will we discover what necessity drives the Lost Ones. Repeatedly, we are reminded that everything in the story, from the dimensions of the cylinder to the behaviour of its people, exists only as a narrative object at the whims of its narrator. Recurring phrases such as, 'for the sake of harmony', 'seen from a certain angle', 'always assuming', and 'if this notion is maintained', clearly subordinate story to narrator. More than once he insists on his omniscience in contrast to the ignorance of his creatures: '. . . to perceive it one must be in the secret of the gods' (p. 19). He leaves no doubt that the customs of the Lost Ones, far from being anthropological relics, derive directly from him. The convention concerning the use of ladders, for example, deals less with the climbers than with the need of the narrative world for harmony. The plight of climbers unable to ascend is less disturbing than the prospect of ladders unable to fulfill a function designated by the narrative: 'Not to mention the intolerable presence of properties serving no purpose' (p. 23). The very form of a cylinder has long been associated with Beckett's narrators. Moran, hampered by stiff knees, retrieves his scattered keys by 'rolling over and over, like a great cylinder' (*Molloy*, p. 153). Malone describes the precious pencil with which he writes as 'a long cylinder' (*Malone*, p. 223), and the narrator in 'The Calmative' sees himself reflected in a shop window as 'a great cylinder sweeping past as though on rollers on the asphalt'.[3] In this context, the phrase 'in the cylinder' refers to the narrator's own mind, and indeed *The Lost Ones* strengthens this connection.

The light in the cylinder corresponds perfectly to the narrator's omniscience. It illumines every surface, including the interior of the tunnels:

... this light is further unusual in that far from evincing one or more visible or hidden sources it appears to emanate from all sides and to permeate the entire space as though this were uniformly luminous down to its least particle of ambiant air. To the point that the ladders themselves seem rather to shed than to receive light with this slight reserve that light is not the word. No other shadows then than those cast by the bodies pressing on one another wilfully or from necessity. . . (pp. 39–40).

This strange light appears frequently in Beckett's work, and has attracted the attention of critics. The *locus classicus* appears in *Malone Dies* where '. . . all bathes . . . in a kind of leaden light that makes no shadow, so that it is hard to say from what direction it comes, for it seems to come from all directions at once, and with equal force' (*Malone*, p. 220). The similarities between this and the longer passage quoted above are striking; both note the absence of shadows, the lack of a definite source, and the uniformity of illumination. When Malone admits 'all that must be half imagination' (p. 185), the link with the cylinder grows clearer, for *The Lost Ones* gives tremendous emphasis to imagination as the power to see what eyesight cannot: 'mental or imaginary frontiers invisible to the eye of flesh' (p. 43), 'imaginary line' (p. 11), 'may be imagined extinguished' (p. 15), 'imaginary edge' (p. 29).

This, then, is the light of the imagination. It is uniform because nothing imagined is hidden to the imagination. Everything receives equal emphasis as in the world of dream. For an imaginary being, to be imagined is all there is to being. There are no other angles; the object, unlike those of the real or waking world, is contained by its appearance: 'all known', as the narrator, describing a similarly lit interior, says in 'Ping'.

From Beckett's view of imagination, we can measure just how far his art has moved beyond Romanticism. The Romantic imagination, in recreating Nature by means of projected images, gives the self new scope for expression and expansion through exploring its relation to that recreated world. But with Beckett this function of imagination is no longer possible, for the two poles of self and world have become inaccessible. Imagination now has nothing but its own futility to express, nothing to project but the emptiness of the assumptions that once linked self and world, and gave experience definite meaning by allowing it to unfold in a stable context. This truth is powerfully expressed in 'Imagination Dead Imagine' where fluctuates the same light as we found in *The Lost Ones*. Conditions such as light and heat that imagination usually takes for granted are pitted against their contraries, dark and cold. In other ways, too, Beckett eliminates the axioms which nourish imagination. Hence, the faces glimpsed in 'Imagination Dead Imagine' entail a number of expectations, such as having two compatible sides: 'The faces too, assuming the two sides of a piece, seem to want nothing essential.'[5] The voice, despite its careful distance, cannot avoid some ambiguity. Does 'want' refer only to a judgement about the correct appearance of the faces or does the word refer to a feeling, a subjective 'want'? A kindred ambiguity in *The Lost Ones* gives us a clearer idea of the only kind of want or need still available for imaginative projection. When discussing the light and temperature, the narrator will not consider any change in their respective oscillations: 'But that would not answer the need of the cylinder. So all is for the best' (p. 42). The ambiguity of 'the needs of the cylinder' emerges near the conclusion where the narrator, projecting 'the unthinkable end', observes that, though only one searching body remains, the light and temperature still fluctuate with the old rhythm: 'But the persistence of the twofold vibration suggests that all is not yet quite for the best' (p. 61). Here it is obvious that 'the needs of the cylinder' concern the narrator and not the inhabitants. All is for the best when the oscillation finally stops forever and his story can end. More precisely, all is for the best when he can turn his hyper-conscious experience of Nothing into an experience of absence such as the vanquished enjoy. That is the narrator's greatest need but one which, as we shall see, can never be satisfied.

The task of imagination, then, in these later works of Beckettian fiction is a little different from that in the previous ones. Where earlier Beckett sought ways to express the experience of Nothing from the inside as it were, as a lived flux with no personal centre, now he tries to express it from the outside by means of images which communicate an experience with less and less content until reaching a state of complete absence. This is the only goal left to imagination and one whose utter impoverishment renders even more vivid the experience of Nothing it tries to escape.[6]

The strategy by which absence is approached in *The Lost Ones* provides a remarkable example of Beckett's consistency. The violent opposition of contraries (light, dark, hot, cold) in the cylinder as well as in 'Imagination Dead Imagine' derives from Beckett's early essay on Joyce's *Work in Progress* where he dusts off Vico's doctrine (borrowed from Bruno) of the coincidence of contraries. An analysis of this doctrine will both disclose the nature of the necessity impelling the seekers and connect this necessity with the narrator's own need for absence:

> The maxima and minima of particular contraries are one and indifferent. Minimal heat equals minimal cold. Consequently transmutations are circular. The principle (minimum) of one contrary takes its movement from the principle (maximum) of another. Therefore not only do the minima coincide with the minima, the maxima with the maxima, but the minima with the maxima in the succession of transmutations. Maximal speed is a state of rest. The maximum of corruption and the minimum of generation are identical: in principle, corruption is generation.[7]

The Lost Ones demonstrates this principle. Each contrary generates its opposite (e.g. hot turning cold) with such rapidity that the contraries in 'the succession of transmutations' do coincide. The contrary prevailing at any given moment can make no difference to the Lost Ones as it will be cancelled out in the next. If each contrary in turn evokes its opposite so that no given moment is specially significant, then the only thing of 'ultimate importance' is the succession itself.

Now, the successions of light, dark, hot, and cold are not the most important ones in the cylinder. That place of

honour is reserved for the contraries of 'languor' (p. 15) and
'fevering' (p. 31) or restless movement of which the others
are analogues. The succession here is realised through individuals but its goal is not dependent on any of them. Beckett
in the Joyce essay explains: 'Thus we have the spectacle of
a human progression that depends for its movement on
individuals in virtue of what appears to be a preordained
cyclicism.'[8] As the word 'preordained' suggests, the cycle is
not purposeless; the end toward which it laboriously tends
is contained in its beginning. Beckett quotes with approval
Joyce's remarks: 'The Vico road goes round and round to
meet where terms begin.'[9] The cycle is consummated when
the contraries causing its revolutions are finally resolved by
the dominance of one over the other. Such precisely is
described by the last sentence of *The Lost Ones;* the languor
in the beginning prevails at the end: 'So much roughly
speaking for the last state of the cylinder and this little
people of searchers one first of whom if a man in some
unthinkable past for the first time bowed his head if this
notion is maintained.' It now becomes clear why the only
goal of seeking is to go on seeking. As the contrary of languor
or abandonment, seeking seeks only to maintain itself. The
fact that it eventually disappears arises not from its own
deficiency, but from the cycle in which it occurs.

The protracted cycle involves, beyond the Lost Ones,
the endless round of stories through which the Beckettian
narrator hopes eventually to earn silence or absence. Beckett's
oeuvre, consistently developing its own implications, is what
Neary in *Murphy* calls 'a closed system'. The common
denominator of the works after *Watt* is the awareness that
the fiction is caught in a cycle of repetition. Starting with the
Trilogy, this recognition becomes the moving principle of the
narrator whose story fundamentally concerns the desire to
tell no more. He wishes to escape the necessity that binds him.

The first word of *The Lost Ones,* 'abode', applies of course
to the cylinder, but refers also to the narrator's wish to place
himself inside boundaries so that his story, beginning at its
outer limits, can contract more and more tightly upon its
own centre and come at last to rest. Both the strategy and
the word derive from *The Unnamable.* In trying to establish

'my abode' (*Unnamable,* p. 296), as a place from which he cannot stir, The Unnamable hopes to reach himself at the end of his narrative, for no matter how long the description of his abode goes on, he will still be in it at the end. Since he has already decided that he and the abode were created simultaneously ('. . . the place was made for me and I for it, at the same instant . . .' (*Unnamable,* p. 296), it follows that, if he can only remain within the walls, he and the abode will end in the same breath. The Beckettian narrator has no fonder wish than this. In *The Lost Ones,* we can easily determine that the 'abode' is built primarily for its narrator, because the cylinder and its inhabitants, he tells us, were created in the same instant, 'In the beginning' (p. 34).

Unfortunately, ever since Mr Knott's house in *Watt,* the Beckettian narrator has not been able to conceal that his abode is merely a patchwork of hypotheses and improvised questions about a meaningless experience. Watt toils with his 'series of hypotheses' (*Watt,* p. 78), Molloy admits, 'For my part I willingly asked myself questions' (*Molloy,* p. 49), and The Unnamable rattles off a salvo of 'Questions, hypotheses, call them that' (*Unnamable,* p. 291). With *The Lost Ones* the narrator feels secure in his abode. As long as he remains inside, the hypotheses by which it is built can be multiplied indefinitely: 'To these questions and many more the answers are clear and easy to give' (p. 52). But continuing a story has never been a problem to the Beckettian narrator; to end and never be obliged to begin again, that is his hope. The silent dark at the conclusion of *The Lost Ones* cannot be, however, any less provisional than the narrative hypothesis from which it springs and which the last five words of the story invoke again: '. . . if this notion is maintained'.

From this point of view, *The Lost Ones* is a story about the narrator's fabrication and dismissal of yet another narrative hypothesis. The contrary states of seeking and abandonment refer ultimately to the endless narrative cycle of pursuing a theme and discarding it in which he is caught. Each ended story leaves the narrator a little more impoverished, whittles down the range of seeking by increasing the scope of abandonment. The word 'abandon' comes directly from the warning written above the entrance to Dante's *Inferno:*

'Abandon all hope ye who enter.' Mr Conaire, in *Mercier and Camier,* clinches the connection: 'I was about to go, said Mr Conaire, all hope abandoned' (*Mercier,* p. 62). The zoned world of the Lost Ones suggests more than simply the Inferno, however. Consider this passage: 'Fourthly those who do not search or non-searchers sitting for the most part against the wall in the attitude which wrung from Dante one of his rare wan smiles' (p. 14). Here Beckett alludes wryly to Dante's bemusement at Belacqua's lethargic pose in the Antechamber to Purgatory (*Purgatorio,* Canto IV). Hence, the cylindrical universe of the Lost Ones, with its emphasis on the two concentric circles in the arena bounded in burn by the circular walls, becomes a highly compresssed, geometrical version of the purposeless, Dantesque universe inhabited by Mercier and Camier. Just as for that 'pseudo-couple' so for the Lost Ones Hell, Purgatory, and Paradise coincide in an empty and meaningless cycle.

This plunging of his narrator ever deeper into an endless and meaningless cycle is one of the chief means by which Beckett transforms his works into a singularly unified tradition whose meaning deepens with each new text. The descent also provides the impetus for Beckett's 'minimal art' — expressing the experience of Nothing within increasingly severe limitations, shrinking narration down to the Nothing it tries to reflect. Malone, for example, speaks of abandonment in terms that explicitly anticipate the vocabulary of *The Lost Ones:* 'And a little less well endowed with strength and courage he too would have abandoned and despaired of ever knowing what manner of being he was, and how he was going to live, and lived vanquished, blindly, in a mad world, in the midst of strangers' (*Malone,* p. 193). The Unnamable reveals that these strangers are the very words he speaks ('. . . I'm all these words, all these strangers . . , *Unnamable,* p. 386) and then predicts a further descent: '. . . they're going to abandon me' (p. 414). Of course, he is right, for *How It Is,* 'Ping'. *Lessness,* and *The Lost Ones* all unfold within restrictive verbal boundaries. Yet the situation is even bleaker than this. As long as the dwindling cycle lasts, the law of the coincidence of contraries applies, and thus seeking *is* abandonment. Such, for example, is The Unnamable's position; knowing that he always seeks and that he will never know why: '... what do I seek now...' (*Unnamable*, p. 387). It is also the case in *The Lost Ones* where the narrator sees his own seeking reflected in a story of abandonment.

The narrator tries to turn this cycle of abandonment to his advantage by running it down to an absolute end. The ploy derives unmistakeably from a passage in *The Unnamable:*

> ... perhaps a whole people is here, and the voice its voice, coming to me fitfully, we would have lived, been free a moment, now we talk about it, each one to himself, each one out loud for himself, and we listen, a whole people, talking and listening, all together, that would ex, no, I'm alone, perhaps the first, or perhaps the last, talking alone, listening alone, alone alone, the others are gone, they have been stilled, their voices stilled, their listening stilled, one by one ... I won't be the last, I'll be with the others, I'll be as gone, in the silence ... it's a lie, I can't stir, I haven't stirred, I launch the voice, I hear a voice ... (p. 409).

Here The Unnamable tells the story of the Lost Ones in miniature. In narrating a vanquished world, he hopes somehow to enter it. Unfortunately, that world exists only as long as he speaks of it and, if he stops, it can no longer be there for him to enjoy. *The Lost Ones* pursues the same strategy and falls into the same trap — what might be called the law of the excluded narrator, where the many who finally succumb point back to the one voice that can never go silent. Unable to find the peace granted his creatures, he is the true Lost One.

The Beckettian Narrator in *Six Stories* and *Nouvelles*

Beckett's stories and *nouvelles* are told by the same futile voice that utters all his fiction. We do not find in these shorter pieces anything not spoken in the longer ones, but they do in some ways provide us with an even more intimate picture of the narrator than can his more elaborate constructions. This happens because stories require far less apparatus than novels. Consequently, we can see even more sharply how narration is manipulated to serve the narrator's needs. Of course, success is no easier here than with his other utterances. Far from releasing him from telling another, each story points to the long intermittent one he is really telling, the one that goes on forever unable to end, forever returning to its impossible beginning:

> When I am abroad in the morning, I go to meet the sun, and in the evening, when I am abroad, I follow it, till I am down among the dead. I don't know why I told this story. I could just as well have told another. Perhaps some other time I'll be able to tell another. Living souls, you will see how alike they are.[1]

He puts this even more starkly at the end of 'The End': 'The memory came faint and cold of the story I might have told, a story in the likeness of my life, I mean without the courage to end or the strength to go on.'[2]

In fact, with their occasional cross-references the six stories we shall examine are better considered as an indefinite series than as wholly independent narrations. The mention at the beginning of 'The Calmative' of 'the night, when the sky with all its lights fell upon me'[3] derives from the closing of 'The End' where 'The sea, the sky, the mountains and the islands closed in and crushed me in a mighty systole, then scattered to the uttermost confines of space' (p. 72). The mention of a 'kepi' in 'First Love'[4] points back to a similar usage in 'The End' (p. 53), while the memory of a hat in 'First Love' has further echoes: 'I wrote somewhere, They gave me . . . a hat. Now the truth is they never gave me a hat, I have always had my own hat, the one my father gave me, and I have never had any other hat than that hat' ('Love', p. 23). The passage recalls both the opening of 'The End' where a charitable organisation gives the narrator a new hat and a section early in 'The Expelled' where the narrator reminisces about his father's purchase of his son's first and only hat.

To express his inability to escape this narrative series, the narrator employs an important image borrowed from another part of the Beckettian canon: narration becomes a 'hell of stories' (*Unnamable*, p. 380). The figure allows him to evoke at once the torment of such a state, the vague hope that someone put him there, and the despair of ever emerging. The Text narrator expresses the lattermost in his pitiful allusion to the very end of the *Inferno* where Dante and Virgil depart from Hell: '. . . we climbed up, he first and I second, so far that I saw through a round opening some of the fair things that Heaven bears; and thence we came forth again to see the stars.'[5] Dante's rejoicing is quite beyond the narrator's grasp: '. . . if I could say, There's a way out there, there's a way out somewhere, the rest would come, the other words, sooner or later, and the power to get there, and the way to get there, and pass out, and see the beauties of the skies, and see the stars again' (*Texts*, p. 121). In the stories, the narrator adopts this notion of damnation by hinting frequently that he is dead: 'I don't know when I died' ('Calmative', p. 27) and '. . . I have never had any other hat than that hat. I may add it has followed me to the grave' ('Love', p. 23). The latter is ambiguous because the story opens in a graveyard.

Hell symbolises the problem of narration, yet it turns out that the stories themselves become extended metaphors for the difficulty of telling them. Beckettian narration is an allegory of its own impediment. The recurrent pattern of expulsion, seeking, falling, and temporary refuge alludes to the narrator's inability to tell a story that will let him end. Every journey returns him to the same need to go on. The stairs which figure so prominently in 'The Expelled' (there are probably more steps in Beckett's *oeuvre* than in the dome of the Vatican) provide an excellent example. They suggest the impossibility of anything but going on with the same vain effort to conclude:

> There were not many steps. I had counted them a thousand times, both going up and coming down, but the figure has gone from my mind. I have never known whether you should say one with your foot on the sidewalk, two with the following foot on the first step, and so on, or whether the sidewalk shouldn't count. At the top of the steps I fell foul of the same dilemma. In the other direction . . . it was the same. The word is not too strong. I did not know where to begin nor where to end, that's the truth of the matter ('Expelled', p. 9).

The stories, however, are not merely allegories. They are intended also to endow the narrator vicariously with self and world so that he will not have to narrate any more. His demands for a world are modest but insistent. Whenever a given narrative setting begins to dissolve, he must desperately forge another. A good example occurs in 'The Calmative'. In the midst of telling about walking around a small gallery high above the nave of a church and right below the dome, the narrator suddenly finds himself completely alone, with 'the void' ('Calmative', p. 36) on the other side of the parapet. Automatically, he constructs another setting to displace this emptiness:

> When they were gone I called. I completed in haste the round of the gallery. No one. I saw on the horizon, where sky, sea, plain and mountains meet, a few low stars, not to be confused with the fires men light, at night, or that go alight alone. Enough (p. 37).

The last word, 'Enough', recurs throughout Beckett's fiction and refers to the temporarily satisfied need for a world. No matter how bleak his stories may be, they always provide this small solace. As the narrator comments a few lines later, 'I wasn't returning empty-handed, not quite, I was taking back with me the virtual certainty that I was still of this world, of that world too, in a way.' Of course it does the narrator no good merely to fabricate a world; he must inhabit it as well, and for this he needs a body, or at least the vestige of one. Hence, we find references to skulls, heads, mouths, hands, etc. in Beckett's fiction: '. . . we are needless to say in a skull' ('The Calmative', p. 38); 'perhaps we're in a head . . .' (*Texts for Nothing,* p. 82); '. . . a voice like this . . . it seeks me blindly, in the dark, it seeks a mouth, to enter into, who can query it, there is no other, you'd need a head . . .' (*Unnamable,* p. 410). These localities are not to be taken literally; they are simply attempts to compensate for the disconnection of self and world that afflicts Beckettian being. A rather disagreeable example occurs in 'The End' where the narrator, having described a little rowboat abode, must put his fictive body firmly into it: 'To contrive a little kingdom, in the midst of the universal muck, then shit on it, ah that was me all over. The excrements were me too, I know . . . but all the same. Enough . . . (p. 78). Excrement is sufficient proof of body.

From this point of view, it makes no difference what story the narrator tells so long as he fills it with cogent detail. He admits to this tactic in 'First Love': '. . . that's the idea, every particular' (p. 30). Now the narrator recognises that this strategy cannot help him in the present, for the very act of narrating separates him from the world narrated. This knowledge does not deter him. If not in the present, perhaps he can forge some measure of being from the fictional past, what he calls his 'myth'.[6] The point is clearly stated in 'Enough': 'It is then I shall have lived or never.'[7] Amidst such zeal to create history, it is no wonder that we find much evidence that narration is sheer imagination. Sometimes even the narrator is surprised at his own invention, as in 'The Calmative': 'But little by little I got myself out and started walking with short steps among the trees, oh look, trees!' (p. 28). At other times, he chooses not to pursue a particular plot complication, as during his little *tête à tête* with the cabman's wife in 'The Expelled': 'No reason for this to end or go on. Then let it end' (p. 23). The narrator knows full well that, despite their convincing attention to concrete detail, his stories are mere illusions, and so he often balks at continuing the ruse: 'How describe this hat? And why? ('End', p. 11) or 'lush pasture lay before me, nonsuch perhaps, who cares. . .' ('Calmative', p. 29).

Why does he undermine these stories that are supposed to redeem him? The answer reveals a basic principle of narration in these stories and one that we have already encountered in *The Unnamable*. The narrator, at bottom, has no interest in creating the illusion of a real world. He wants instead to prolong the illusion of a dream-world, a world of visions, so that he can hope either to awaken at last to his true self or fall asleep and dream forever. Whereas in later works like *The Lost Ones* and 'Imagination Dead Imagine' we found that the role of imagination was to reduce the narrative world to the Nothing it tries to express, in these stories imagination has the task of inventing dream. We find here much evidence of visions. At any given moment, the narrator may intrude an account of a vision, as in 'The Expelled' immediately after his plunge down the steps ('In a sort of vision I saw the door open and my feet come out,' p. 12) or inside the cab when he pictures the horse ('I saw the horse as with my eyes of flesh,' p. 19). By 'The Calmative' it becomes obvious that narration is no more than a futile attempt of imagination to create a continuous series of dream-visions:

> I see a kind of den littered with empty tins. And yet we are not in the country. Perhaps it's just ruins, a ruined folly, on the skirts of the town, in a field, for the fields come right up to our walls, their walls, and the cows lie down at night in the lee of the ramparts. I have changed refuge so often, in the course of my rout, that now I can't tell between dens and ruins. But there was never any city but the one. It is true you often move along in a dream, houses and factories darken the air, trams go by, and under your feet wet from the grass there are suddenly cobbles (pp. 27–8).

Now we see more clearly why he depends on the stories to give him being in the past, for he can only hope to wake up or fall asleep in some eventual present if they have sustained the dreaming until then. Three stories, 'The Expelled', 'The

Calmative', and 'The End', definitely move toward this goal. The first begins with an expulsion from the common waking world where things are already available to be perceived. The feverish movement of the second, jumping from scene to scene and filled with strange encounters, emphasises that an alternate world is under construction, one which exists only when perceived. The third, with its culminating vision of universal collapse, tries to end both dream and dreamer forever.

The narrator has another reason for constructing a past. If he can build a memory, perhaps he can become him to whom the memory belongs and so find a self at last. In so far as both memory and dream are illusions meant to change the present, there is not much difference between them, and this the Text narrator recognises: 'Will they succeed in slipping me into him, the memory and the dream of me, into him still living. . .' (*Texts*, p. 134). The other three stories, 'First Love', 'Enough', and 'From an Abandoned Work', will illustrate.

The narrator's initial interest in the 'two limiting dates' ('Love', p. 11) of his father's birth and death and his use of the latter to establish a third — that of his own marraige — leave no doubt about the importance of memory in 'First Love'. It turns out that the story deals not with ordinary memory but with the immensely significant one about when the need to narrate began. The first hint of this allegory occurs when the narrator observes that 'what goes by the name of love is banishment' (p. 18). If we remember that the recurrent theme of expulsion and banishment throughout the stories reflects the narrator's own wanderings in telling them, the link between Anna (alias Lulu) and embarking on an endless narrative journey strengthens. In fact, the narrator's flippancy about his mate's name suggests that she is merely an invention, designed to satisfy the need to narrate. By first removing all the furniture from his new room after moving into her apartment, he hints more broadly about his intention to invent: 'such density of furniture defeats imagination' (p. 28).

The changes in the narrator's position before, during, and after his nuptial night in the apartment constitute yet another one of his myths — this time concerning his fall from a more definite being to the marginal one he now endures. Before meeting Anna, he is a barren enough figure to be sure, but neither depends upon nor seeks anything beyond himself. This situation alters rapidly once he makes contact with her. He can no longer rest, and craves release from his tormented self: 'To be nothing but pain, how that would simplify matters!' (p. 20). During the marriage night his state further deteriorates, and he begins already to resemble the Beckettian narrator he really is. Words break in suddenly upon him unrelated to any object ('I heard the word fibrome . . .' p. 29) or any subject ('Never had my voice taken so long to reach me as on this occasion,' p. 31). It is extremely significant that the sexual consummation which will have such important consequences after he wakes actually occurs while he sleeps. The same problem arises here as when the Text narrator asks, 'How are the intervals filled between these apparitions?' (*Texts,* p. 101) or when The Unnamable muses, 'I think I must have blackouts' (*Unnamable,* p. 368). Without a genuine self, the Beckettian narrator has no means of grasping or accounting for the continuity of his own experience. Deep sleep, intervals, blackouts — these are all hypotheses that, even as they perform the unifying function of a self, point to the lack of one. By setting the principle phase of his transformation in the midst of a deep sleep, the narrator of 'First Love' bases upon an unverifiable hypothesis the most critical moment of his life. By not taking personal responsibility for his experience, he is denying responsibility for himself. Some months later, a baby is born and the narrator's uncertainty whether it is his is really an uncertainty whether he is himself. Indeed, we soon see that he no longer has a self at all. The birth cries finally drive him from the house, but he still hears them ever fainter, each time he halts:

> As long as I kept walking I didn't hear them, because of the footsteps. But as soon as I halted I heard them again, a little fainter each time, admittedly, but what does it matter, faint or loud, cry is cry, all that matters is that it should cease. For years I thought they would cease. Now I don't think so anymore (pp. 35—6).

The cries presage those which disturb The Unnamable whenever the voice stops:

> ... the words fail, the voice fails, so be it, I know that well,
> it will be the silence, full of murmurs, distant cries, the
> usual silence, spent listening, spent waiting, waiting for the
> voice ... (*Unnamable,* p. 413).

Even on a quick reading, the two passages closely resemble
one another. When we remember that the narrator of the first
passage only hears the cries when he is not moving and that
movement is itself a symbol of narrating, the passages look
yet more alike. In both, the narrator is expressing his inability to be himself in silence, and 'First Love' is the allegory
of how this inability began.

Similarly, in 'Enough' the narrator fashions a remembered
and allegorical past in order to fix some kind of personal
identity in the present or, more precisely, to provide some
account of the act of narrating through which he is. Since, as
we have already seen, this narrative act is never fulfilled but
goes on forever seeking an unattainable consummation, the
narrator can never account adequately for it in direct or
literal terms. To prove this statement, we have only to consider *The Unnamable* and *Texts for Nothing* where the attempt to narrate the act of narration, to give a perfect trans-
cription of narration ('I say it as I hear it'), turns out to be a
task with no end and hence with no meaning. Thus, the
narrator runs headlong into a paradox: he can only claim a
self through grasping the act of narration but that very act,
by going on endlessly in search of an unavailable conclusion,
expresses his inability ever to do so. The closest the narrator
can come to having an identity is to reflect his lack of one.
For that task allegory is well suited.

On a casual reading, 'Enough' simply concerns the past
wanderings of the narrator (this time using a female persona — the only one in Beckett's fiction) with an aged and
faltering man. Even on this literal level their journey is
obviously a narrative one, for the old man dictates as they
creep forward. But this is not the only level. In the first
place, the story breaks into two distinct parts: (1) a single
paragraph introduction which narrates the present, and (2)
the story proper. The introduction is especially interesting
for, employing the favourite tactic of another narrating per-

sona, Malone, it stresses the relationship between pen and writer:

> All that goes before forget. Too much at a time is too much. That gives the pen time to note. I don't see it but I hear it there behind me. Such is the silence. When the pen stops I go on. Sometimes it refuses. When it refuses I go on. Too much silence is too much. Or it's my voice too weak at times. The one that comes out of me. So much for the art and craft (p. 53).

We cannot avoid the impression that the story which follows is a reverse image of this introduction: the female narrator becomes the pen and the old man, the hand and mind propelling it. Emphasis is given to his hand holding hers and to the gradual transformation of his posture from that of an erect man to that of a hand running over paper ('In the end his trunk ran parallel with the ground,' p. 55). Moreover, both the introduction concerning pen and writer and the story itself describe a couple alternately stopping and going on while listening to a voice. Why, though, does the narrator tell a story that suggests the one a pen might write of the hand that moves it?

To answer we must first notice that the introductory paragraph about pen and narrating 'I' ends with the curious sentence: 'So much for the art and craft.' The last three words derive from the end of a passage in *Three Dialogues with Georges Duthuit* (quoted in Chapter 6) referring to the lack of a manageable relation between the two terms, self and world:

> My case, since I am in the dock, is that van Velde is the first to desist from this esthetized automatism, the first to submit wholly to the incoercible absence of relation, in the absence of terms or, if you like, in the presence of unavailable terms, the first to admit that to be an artist is to fail, as no other dare fail, that failure is his world and the shrink from it desertion, *art and craft* [my italics], good housekeeping, living.[8]

The remark 'So much for the art and craft' alerts us, then, that the story will involve the impossibility of finding the two terms, self and world. Indeed, the relation between the female persona and the old man indicates that no true subject can be found. Like all Beckettian couples, they are barely separable as subjects. Even their needs coincide: 'We must have had the same satisfactions. The same needs and the same satisfactions' (p. 53). Yet, they are sufficiently distinct that the needs of the old man precede and determine those of his companion. Such redundancy is precisely the function of the Beckettian couple. The initiative of one allows the other to act so that they imitate (we can hardly say 'constitute') a single subject.

By thus implying that pen and hand are just another couple improvising a false subjectivity, the narrator develops an allegory about his biggest problem: the impossibility of knowing who is narrating. The familiar situation of one voice narrating and a pen (or another voice) recording expresses once again the narrator's inability to grasp his own subjectivity. But he does get some compensation. Through this story and its female persona, he places himself in a past world, even if that world only reflects his separation from his own inaccessible subjectivity, his separation from the voice he hears. The word 'enough' serving as title and appearing repeatedly in the story indicates, as we saw earlier, the need to create some world where he can be. These myths of world and body are his calmatives, and bareness certainly does not detract from their utility:

> We were on the whole calm. More and more. All was. This notion of calm comes from him. Without him I would not have had it. Now I'll wipe out everything but the flowers. No more rain. No more mounds. Nothing but the two of us dragging through the flowers. Enough my old breasts feel his old hand ('Enough', p. 60).

Like the other two stories, 'From an Abandoned Work' relies on memory to develop an allegory of narration. Here the narrator gives himself a more sympathetic past than elsewhere in his utterances. Though the three days he describes are 'awful'[9] enough, the emotional world in which they unfold is not completely removed from the one we know. As the narrator observes, the adolescent boy recalled in the story is 'just strange' (p. 44) and still a part of the small society around him. His relationship with his mother, for example, has none of the buffoonery that governs Molloy's interviews with the woman that bore him. Nevertheless, he leaves no doubt that these memories are contrived and cannot be sustained: '. . . there was never anything, never can be, life and death all nothing, that kind of thing, only a voice dreaming and droning on all around. . .' (p. 49). This admission is part of a cunning strategy, for the narrator wants the sequence of remembered days to express, not a literal past, but an endless series whose parts are all alike: 'But let me get on now with the day I have hit on to begin with, any other would have done as well, yes, on with it and out of my way and on to another. . .' (p. 40). Each story is like another day to get through in a pointless and endless life. In abandoning, as the title indicates, the impossible task of telling the story of his life, the narrator dismisses, as in *How It Is,* the conventions and beliefs by which time and experience are given definite order and direction. He thus expresses the experience of Nothing where moments cling together in the same void and no clarifying principle of continuity can be found.

Aside from referring to the bibliographical fact that Beckett salvaged this story from a much longer, unpublished fragment, the word 'abandoned' applies to the narrator in a second way. The story itself, as an attempt to create a world and body that the narrator can inhabit, is abandoned like all the others. The full extent of this abandonment emerges in connection with a passage from 'Afar a Bird', published by Beckett nineteen years later in 1976:

> . . . I'll put faces in his head, names, places, churn them all up together, all he needs to end, phantoms to flee, last phantoms, to flee and to pursue, he'll confuse his mother with whores, his father with a roadman named Balfe . . .[10]

The 'roadman named Balfe' appears in 'From an Abandoned Work', and thus it becomes clear that the unusually sensitive narrator of that story is himself but another persona of the Beckettian narrator. Now, the persona has an 'I' only in so far as he narrates his adolescence filled with faces, names, and places. Omit the past and that 'I' which seems so vivid and emotional would instantly have no one to be, would be no one. Yet, the narrator behind him is in an even more precarious position. His persona can have subjectivity only in virtue of a 'myth', but the narrator has subjectivity only in virtue of his phantoms, the personae. In these stories therefore, the narrator is no more than a series of 'apparitions'[11] (the word used by the Text narrator) manifesting his own lack of self and world. We can only marvel at Samuel Beckett who, through his beleaguered narrator, pushes ever closer to expressing the coincidence of two impossible contraries: Being and Nothing.

10

Fizzles

On each of his journeys, whether tranquil or frantic, the Beckettian narrator attempts a different way of reflecting himself, or better, his lack of self. In *Murphy* his glass is the closed narrative system that has no ultimate subject; in *Watt*, the wholly hypothetical world inhabited by the hero; in *Mercier and Camier*, the couple in their futile effort to preserve subjectivity; in the Trilogy, the voice of species powerless to become an individual; in *Texts for Nothing*, the expression of his own impossibility; in *How It Is*, the fiction of time; in *The Lost Ones*, the stillness of the vanquished. Underlying these diverse reflections is a profound uncertainty about their accuracy, their fitness to duplicate the errant subject. Consequently, each one of those works is strewn with questions that touch every aspect of narration from the identity of the narrator (as with The Unnamable's 'Who now?' *Unnamable*, p. 291) to the purpose and nature of his story ('What am I to do, what shall I do, what should I do, in my situation, how proceed?' *Unnamable*, p. 291). Nowhere in these books is the narrator at ease with his ignorance. He may, as in *Texts for Nothing*, reach a provisional resignation, but even there his most ringing statements are never very far from another hypothesis or query. Indeed, the word, 'strange', recurs in the works, not with the insistence of words, like 'nothing', 'no', 'never', or 'voice', yet often enough to remind us that, far from learning or adapting, the narrator remains bewildered by his predicament.

The situation changes sharply with *For To End Yet Again and Other Fizzles* published in 1976. Here the narrator, still tinkering with mirrors, is no longer unsure of what he sees in them. Though filled with the old negations and denials, he

118

speaks in a new tone of voice that amounts, if not to a reconciliation with his plight, at least to a confirmation of his resolve to bear it. We hear this in the opening phrase, 'For to end yet again' — unexpectant, determined, resilient. We hear it again in a reminiscence mingling fact with perhaps a trace of sentiment: '. . . Murphy had first-rate legs.'[1] After all his false starts and falser endings, the narrator now admits what he can never have doubted: narration will get him nowhere but to a clearer vision of what he already is. Despite some similarity he is not doing here what he attempts in *Texts for Nothing,* for there he projects himself as pure hypothesis with only enough being to pose the question of his own identity. Here, on the other hand, and for the first time in any of the works, he asks not a single question as there is no longer anything to be answered. He has at last grown familiar with his own absence and wants now to say so.

The first Fizzle (entitled 'For To End Yet Again') pushes expression further than ever before toward the ineffable assimilation of being by Nothing. The opening lines clearly focus on these two contraries:

> For to end yet again skull alone in a dark place pent bowed on a board to begin. Long thus to begin till the place fades followed by the board long after. For to end yet again skull alone in the dark the void no neck no face just the box last place of all in the dark the void (p. 11).

Here the two contraries are reduced to the simple opposition of place with its contents on the one hand and 'the dark the void' on the other. Even in this brief passage, we can see place rapidly fading into Nothing, but the former is never entirely extinguished. Narration approaches the coincidence of the minimum of being with the maximum of Nothing. All the elements connected with place express the last remains of dwindling subjectivity — the skull, the board (an old accessory for the narrator),* the box (reminder of the death he seeks in order to prove his life). The narrator makes the connection between place and impoverished being explicit: 'Place of remains where once used to gleam in the dark on

*See above, p. 51.

and off used to glimmer a remain' (p. 11). Elements in this sentence strongly echo the passage from 'Peintres de l'empêchement' treating an absent subject that we examined in Chapter VI:† 'an isolated being, enclosed and shut up forever in itself, without trace, without air, Cyclopean, glimpsed midst lightning flashes and spectral shades of black.') There are several more echoes in the same Fizzle: 'grey timeless air' (p. 12) and 'hell air' (p. 15) recall 'without air' while 'Atop the Cyclopean brow' recalls 'Cyclopean'.[2] The dwarf couple that soon come into view have the same task of rescuing subjectivity that all Beckettian couples pursue, and hence there is no distinction between them as agents: 'From time to time impelled as one they let fall the litter then again as one take it up again without having to stoop' (p. 13). The use of words, some of them frequently repeated, such as 'remain', 'end', 'ruin', and 'by degrees', indicates that the narrator regards his problem of impoverishment as an endless diminishing cycle. This seems a much more courageous position than that taken in *The Lost Ones* where the cycle runs down to a definite but spurious terminus.

This comparison with the earlier work will help us. Just as we found *The Lost Ones* primarily to concern the predicament of the narrator imagining it, so 'For To End Yet Again' underscores the power of imagination to represent what otherwise cannot be seen: 'invisible to any other eye' (p. 11), 'so alike the eye cannot tell them apart' (p. 12), 'to imagine if he can see it' (p. 13), 'Then on so soft the eye does not see them' (p. 14). Whereas in *The Lost Ones* the imagination tries at last to place the narrator in an abandoned world which he will never have to leave, the last sentence of 'For To End Yet Again' declares that such a happy ending can never occur: 'Through it who knows yet another end beneath a cloudless sky same dark it earth and sky of a last end if ever there had to be another absolutely had to be' (p. 15). The change is perhaps not so courageous as might appear. In *Fizzles*, imagination goes beyond minimal art, beyond reduction to zero, and instead has the task now of maintaining some contact with a subjective pole, however vague.

†See above, p. 74.

This must be done lest the experience of Nothing, void of all
relation to subjectivity, lapse into a vacancy so absolute that
it can no longer be called an experience at all. Accordingly,
we find in *Fizzles* different ways of improvising subjectivity
in the face of Nothing. One of these ways is to preserve some
distance between the experience of Nothing and the report-
ing of it. Hence, we find both a looking at Nothing ('He
facing forward will sometimes hold and hoist as best he can
his head as if to scan the void and who knows alter course,'
pp. 13–14) and, through the cited passages concerning the
imagination, a looking at that looking. The same thing
happens in the Fizzle, 'Still', where the persona sits before
a window 'staring out at nothing' (p. 20) while in turn stared
at by the narrator ('. . . closer inspection namely detail by
detail. . . .' p. 20). The theme is given geometrical expression
in the Fizzle, 'Closed Space'. Here three elements are stressed:
a 'place consisting of an arena and a ditch' (p. 49), the
Nothing that stretches all around ('Beyond what is said there
is nothing,' p. 49 and 'Beyond the ditch there is nothing'),
and the perspective on the place ('Seen from the edge. . . ,
p. 49). It soon becomes obvious, through one sentence very
strongly echoing that now familiar passage in 'Peintres de
l'empêchement', that the place described in a symbol of an
absent or inaccessible subjectivity: 'In the black air towers of
pale light' (p. 50). Indeed, the narrator seems almost to have
borrowed from Beckett's description of Bram van Velde's
painting.

Each of these three Fizzles, then, reduces the scope of
witnessing so drastically that only the merest distinction
obtains between the witness and Nothing. A fourth Fizzle,
'He Is Barehead', is the most audacious of all, for there the
narrator actually constructs subjectivity bit by bit from
astonishingly frugal material. I find this Fizzle remarkable,
because it states more vividly than anywhere else the narrator's
experience of Nothing and his desperate need to precipitate
a self from that experience. He places the barehead persona
in a dark labyrinth of cold stone. Wandering in such a place is
a vivid symbol for his own narrative difficulties, reaching the
end of one story only to begin another ('This is the end of
the road, nothing now but to return to the other terminus

and start again,' p. 26) or thinking that he has finally begun the last story only to find that the old one still continues: 'And often he suddenly begins, in these black windings, and makes his first steps for quite a while before realizing they are merely the last or latest' (p. 29). This dim world reflects as closely as possible the narrator's own lack of one, but the persona nevertheless manages to accumulate experiences in it worthy of a subject. At the beginning he does not know how he entered such a place, but 'little by little his history took shape. . .' (p. 29). The process, like the reverse one in the first Fizzle, procedes by insensible degrees with the man stumbling up and down narrow corridors until he gains memories to call his own: '. . . such as the straitest narrow, the loudest fall, the most lingering collapse, the steepest descent, the greatest number of successive turns the same way, the greatest fatigue, the longest rest, the longest — except for the sound of body on its way — silence' (pp. 29–30). By the end, the persona acquires a vast number of discrete experiences, but we must recognise that only through memory can he do so. Only by remembering experience can he grasp how varied that experience is.

It turns out, therefore, that this Fizzle is a deceiving reflection of the narrator's own experience of Nothing which never varies at all and which, like the night passed in sleep, 'has no parts' (*Unnamable,* p. 407). The narrator looks at an image of himself in the distorting mirror of memory not only to glimpse a past on which to hang his personal identity, but also in order that he may have separable experiences, and gain some relief from a single, unbroken one. Without memory, the barehead persona in the labyrinth would be in the same position as The Unnamable whose lament measures the abyss between the ability to order experience and the impossibility of ever doing so: 'Labyrinthine torment that can't be grasped, or limited, or felt, of suffered, no, not even suffered. . .' (*Unnamable,* p. 314).

The Fizzle, 'Horn Came Always', makes a similar effort to turn the experience of Nothing into one consisting of discrete parts. The narrator imagines himself in a room with a bed (where have we read this before!), visited each night for 'five or six minutes' (p. 34) by his assistant, Horn. Already we recognise the attempt to represent the experience of Nothing, for the room is completely dark, and Horn, occasionally shining a light on his notes to find whatever 'particular' (p. 34) the narrator seeks, is no more than an expression of the narrator's need to fill up his own vacancy with the illusion of concrete detail and, even more important, the passage of time. He readily admits to the latter: 'These allusion to now, to before and after, and all such yet to come, that we may feel ourselves in time' (p. 33).[3] One night the narrator's curiosity drives him to commit the same error that ended Cupid's tryst with Psyche: he causes his visitor's face to be illuminated. When the room is finally dark again, the apparition of Horn's face 'unaccountably . . . lingered on' (p. 34) until the narrator can no longer determine whether the experience is real, hallucinatory, or imaginary. This gets too close for comfort to the genuine experience of Nothing, so he hastily turns his attention to his body (another illusion as we saw in Chapter 9), concluding with one of his more extravagantly concrete testimonies:

> What ruined me at bottom was athletics. With all that jumping and running when I was young, and even long after in the case of certain events, I wore out the machinery before its time. My fortieth year had come and gone and I still throwing the javelin (p. 35).

Where many of these Fizzles protect the experience of Nothing from complete evacuation and consequent extinction by maintaining marginal contact with a subjective pole or, at least, with the concept of time necessary to this pole, two other Fizzles, 'Afar a Bird' and 'I Gave Up Before Birth', express the virtual impossibility of doing so. Indeed, together they repeat the words 'impossible' and 'possible' fourteen times. Beckett's Fizzles have been compared to chamber music, and the analogy seems especially apt since 'I Gave Up', repeating entire passages from 'Afar a Bird', reads like a coda to its companion.[4] Here, the narrator, by affirming his lack of identity, by admitting that he can never gain that of his persona, acquires nevertheless a kind of negative identity as he whose reflection is not his own: '. . . a life of my own I tried, in vain, never any but his, worth nothing, because of me. . .' (p. 40).

The last Fizzle, 'Old Earth', begins as an address or apostrophe to the earth under which the narrator hopes soon to lie.

> You'll be on me, it will be you, it will be me, it will be us, it was never us. It won't be long now, perhaps not tomorrow, nor the day after, but too late. Not long now, how I gaze on you, and what refusal, now you refuse me, you so refused (p. 53).

It ends with an equally strong yearning for the past (in both cases the word, 'gaze', emphasises the narrator's concentration):

> No but now, now, simply stay still, standing before a window, one hand on the wall, the other clutching your shirt, and see a sky, a long gaze, but no, gasps and spasms, a childhood sea, other skies, another body (p. 54).

Looking forward to death that will not hasten, looking back toward youth that will not return, he is abandoned in a present where past and future refuse to help him, and this in turn in another way of expressing the experience of Nothing. Knowing that Beckett was seventy when he published this Frizzle, I am reminded more poignantly than anywhere else in his fiction of E. M. Cioran's intimation that, underneath all the narrator's utterances, one can catch the inflexions of the author's own speaking voice.[5] Of course, I should immediately add that any attempt to associate Beckett the private man with his fiction is just as precarious as efforts to identify the narrator with his personae. The phrase 'old earth' has already appeared in 'From An Abandoned Work': '. . . often now my murmur falters and dies and I weep for happiness as I go along and for love of this old earth that has carried me so long and whose uncomplainingness will soon be mine' (p. 45). Since we observed earlier that this 'I' is but another persona of the narrator, there is no final justification to treat the 'I' of 'Old Earth' any differently.

Conclusion

Perhaps the most formidable obstacle to approaching Beckett's narrations is the necessity of suspending the expectations which prose fiction as a genre entrains. There is no expectation more entrenched than the one which, deriving from the ancient convention of mimesis, assumes that fiction should reflect, however figuratively and diversely, the experience of life or living. Cleanth Brooks and Robert Penn Warren state this assumption in its most common form:

> When we read a piece of fiction, we move from the world where we, as people, live, into a world of imagination. But that world of imagination has been created by a writer out of the actual world in which he, as a person, lives.[1]

But the notions of life or living, as Beckett insists in a passage already quoted from *Three Dialogues with Georges Duthuit* (see p. 74 and p. 114), are precisely what art can no longer pursue, for they imply a stable relation between two terms, self and world, which are now unavailable and problematic. Even in the second sentence of the above quotation from Brooks and Warren, we can see very clearly how the notion of living ('lives') presupposes a connection between a definite subject (in this example referred to in three ways as 'writer', 'he', and 'person') and his world. Beckett, in contrast, begins with the dissolution or departure of these poles, and undertakes the enormous task of exploring human experience struggling to reconstitute them. To this end, he develops his remarkable narrator who becomes a universal human voice, the voice of species, seeking in the void the certainties of subject and object that once made human experience intelligible. The Beckettian narrator is always careful to distinguish his present experience from the one called life: 'There was never anything, never can be, life and death all nothing' (*From An Abandoned Work,* p. 49). The only life he can claim is that narrated in his fictions of the past: 'It is then I shall have lived or never' ('Enough', p. 57).

Beckett moves the starting point of representation downwards, as it were, toward a stratum of human experience more fundamental than that of individual life shored up by unexamined assumptions. He wants to plumb a region of *human* being whose roots are primordial but whose final emergence is definitively modern — that hypothesising, interpretive urge of the human spirit persisting in the utter absence of the given and hence of knowledge, forced to abandon all comforting structures. In this darkness, human experience is no longer what Husserl calls 'intentional', that is, directed toward objects or structures whose natures are open to exploration, but instead is an awareness of Nothing — issueless, unprecipitated, yet indelibly ours and born of the relentless need to fix the certain poles of experience. It is important to recognise that Beckett's intuition of Nothing has no despair or pessimism in it. Despair and pessimism are attitudes of the self toward life, or, more specifically, toward conditions such as the resistance of history, adverse circumstances, or the inevitability of death, that limit the horizons of life. With Beckett, in contrast, the course of life or what happens in life is far less interesting than what he identifies as the basic human predicament which goes on regardless of the kinds of lives lived.

In expressing his vision, Beckett takes a tremendous risk. On the one hand, as shown earlier in Chapter One, he exploits the structural principles of his chosen medium, narration, by transforming the literal predicament of a narrator caught between the poles of voice and silence into a symbol for the plight of human experience stranded between poles of self and world. But, on the other hand, by focusing so strictly on the structural polarities within narration, Beckett also engages the polarities outside it — namely, reader and author. Here is the last of many paradoxes on which Beckett's art rests: the more he foregrounds the internal poles of narration, the more he inevitably involves the external ones together with the assumptions supporting them. Yet, this involvement is precisely what Beckett's art cannot afford. The moment author and reader, as already intact selves, are included in the closed universe of Beckett's prose fiction, the meaning of that universe changes.

Consider the author first. The temptation to see a given work as a disguised allusion to the life of its author is almost irresistible, but observe what happens when we treat Beckett's work this way. The notion of life posits self and world and moves them through time from birth to death. Hence, to assume that Beckett's work is a reflection of his life is to view his fiction from a perspective that begs all the questions about world, time and personal identity which are raised in his fiction. To inhibit this tendency to identify story with the life of the author, Beckett in many of his works gives us texts whose narrator is in the act of writing them. There is no one else left outside to whom the text might refer or, more exactly, when such contentious references are made, it is clear that they do not apply to the experience being narrated: 'I am far from all that wrangle' (*Texts,* p. 75).

Beckettian narration must avoid also contamination from the other external pole – the reader. Here the situation is far more complex. By its very nature, narration implies the reader as listener, and invites him to complete the text by bringing to it his own subjectivity and experiences of life. As Sartre, for example, writes of *Crime and Punishment,* 'On the one hand, the literary object has no other substance than the reader's subjectivity; Raskolnikov's waiting is *my* waiting which I lend him. Without this impatience of the reader he would remain only a collection of signs.'[2] In first person narration, the type most common in Beckett's prose fiction, the reader's contribution is even more strongly encouraged, since to the conventional first person narrator the experience of narration is, at bottom, an awareness of the reader. Obviously Beckett must suppress the implicit reference to the reader and deflect the reader's consequent tendency to project his own subjectivity onto the text. Otherwise, the reader, assuming that the Beckettian narrator is a self just as he is, will misinterpret the narrator's experience accordingly. Thus, Malone writes just for himself while trying to co-ordinate

death and narrative termination. The function of his emphasis
on pencil and notebook is to push out all reference to author
and reader. Similarly, The Unnamable narrates not to a reading audience but to the void and only in order to find the
words that will let him end.

Indeed, beginning with *Murphy,* the construction of such
closed narrative systems has always fulfilled a dual function
in Beckett's prose fiction: first, to drain narration of all
assumptions about self and world so that the experience of
Nothing might by expressed, and second to emphasise the
boundary between that closed narrative system and the world
of 'life' outside it that we all take for granted and are only
too ready to smuggle into the text. No doubt Beckett is
severe with his readers, demanding — as did Mr Knott with
Watt — that they abandon their ordinary expectations of
meaning in experience before entering his domain. Yet,
whereas Watt gains nothing from his stay but bewilderment
and fatigue, Beckett's readers learn more if they agree to
Beckett's terms. Then, at last, the intense, hypnotic narrator
is heard to speak, not with the voice of self or ego confessing,
as in Dostoevsky's *Notes from Underground,* private, personal doubts we prefer to hide away, but with the urgent
voice of species trying to utter for our age the meaning of
man. Thus, within the confines of Beckett's prose fiction we
circle ever closer toward the perplexing centre of our own
humanity.

Notes

Author's Note The following UK editions correspond to US editions used in the text:

More Pricks Than Kicks, Calder & Boyars, 1970.
Murphy, John Calder, 1969.
Watt, John Calder, 1963.
Mercier and Camier, Calder & Boyars, 1974.
Molloy, John Calder, 1971.
Malone Dies, John Calder, 1968.
The Unnamable, John Calder, 1975.
Texts for Nothing, Calder & Boyars, 1974.
How It Is, John Calder, 1964.
Four Novellas, John Calder, 1978.
Six Residua, John Calder, 1979.

The following US editions correspond to the UK editions used in the text:

Our Exagmination Round his Factification for Incamination of Work in Progress, New Directions, 1972.
Proust, Grove, 1957.
Fizzles, Grove, 1976.
The Lost Ones, Grove, 1972.

CHAPTER 1 (pp. 1–10)

1 Esslin, ed., *Samuel Beckett: A Collection of Critical Essays,* 1.

2 Interpretations of Beckettian self-consciousness: the artist trying to grasp his own creative act: Copeland, *Art and the Artist in the Works of Samuel Beckett;* withdrawal from the world of others through insanity: Bernard, *Samuel Beckett: A New Approach;* withdrawal through impotence: Eugene Webb, for example, regards

129

Texts for Nothing as representing 'a person who can do nothing and who knows he can do nothing'. See his *Samuel Beckett: A Study of his Novels*, 153.

3 Hugh Kenner was the first to explore in detail the link between the narrator and the Cartesian *cogito* — a venerable French invention. See his *Samuel Beckett: A Critical Study* 117—132. His view was anticipated in part by Geneviève Bonnefoi in 'Textes Pour Rien?' *Lettres Nouvelles*, 428, where she places the narrator 'dans le monde indéfini de la pensée à l'état brut'. Her analysis turns the narrator into a kind of nascent or unformed *cogito* trying to constitute its own world of thought. A Hegelian interpretation has been offered by Hans-Joachim Schultz, *This Hell of Stories: A Hegelian Approach to the Novels of Samuel Beckett*. For Kierkegaard see Esslin, 5—8; for Sartre, Hesla, *The Shape of Chaos*, 184—192.

4 A neo-Freudian reading is given by Fernande Saint-Martin, *Samuel Beckett et l'univers de la Fiction*. Saint-Martin shows how psychoanalysis informs the expression of the Beckettian narrator. By descending deeper and deeper into himself, the narrator is trying to understand how his own subjectivity has been influenced by the Oedipal figures of father and mother. He is trying to reintegrate his personal world by defining his identity in his own terms and by fulfilling, in his interior universe, the archetypal functions of father and mother. He is the mother giving the milk of words to his personae; he is the father by eliminating all other authority.

5 Samuel Beckett, *Proust and Three Dialogues with Georges Duthuit*, London: Calder 1965, 103. Other critics have also used this passage to introduce their views, though with very different results. See, for examples, Esslin, 2, Hesla, 4, and Saint-Martin, 15.

6 *Ibid*, 125.

7 *Ibid*, 101.

8 *Three Novels: Molloy; Malone Dies; The Unnamable*, trans. Beckett and Bowles, New York: Grove 1965, 192. Hereafter, reference to specific novels in this Trilogy will be included in the text with the appropriate page num-

ber(s) in parentheses.

9 Beckett, *Murphy,* New York: Grove 1957, 246. Future references to *Murphy* will be included in the text with the appropriate page number(s) in parentheses.

10 Beckett, *Texts for Nothing* in *Stories and Texts for Nothing,* New York: Grove 1967, 157. Future references to this book will appear in the text with the appropriate page number(s) in parentheses.

11 *Three Novels,* 388. Ihab Hassan connects this silence with the eruption of self into literature. Inevitably, there is no longer an Other with whom to communicate. He argues that, through silence, Beckett is expressing self-insulation. See *The Literature of Silence,* 207. In contrast, I think that Beckett goes much further and wants first to establish the silence as the ground for all narration in order then to express the complete absence of the two poles, self and world — a condition far more unstable than mere self-insulation.

CHAPTER 2 (pp. 11–26)

1 For example, see *L'Herne Beckett,* eds Bishop and Federman, 357.

2 Beckett, *More Pricks than Kicks,* 90. All quotations are from the 1974 Pan edition.

3 Hugh Kenner refers to this passage in more general terms: 'There have been few inventions in fiction to compare with the voice from universal space that speaks those three words. It is later, soured and personified, the prevailing voice of the trilogy.' See *Samuel Beckett: A Critical Study,* 49.

4 Alice and Kenneth Hamilton also notice this emphasis on pity. See their *Condemned to Life: The World of Samuel Beckett,* 110.

5 Ruby Cohn, too, has observed that the narrator is no more serious than Belacqua. See *Back to Beckett,* 23.

6 Many critics have noted the absolute dependency of the surrounding characters on Murphy. See, for example, Robinson, *The Long Sonata of the Dead,* 86.

7 David H. Hesla mentions a connection between Murphy and Leibnitz in his *The Shape of Chaos,* 33. For a fas-

cinating, neo-Freudian perspective on Murphy as a monad see Saint-Martin, 29—43.

8 *Monadology,* in Leibnitz, *Discourse on Metaphysics, Correspondence with Arnauld* and *Monadology,* trans. George R. Montgomery, LaSalle Illinois: The Open Court Publishing Company 1962, 252.

9 Wilhelm Windelband, *A History of Philosophy,* vol. 2, trans. James H. Tufts, New York: Harper and Row, 1958, 423, n. 5.

10 Compare Voice B in *That Time:* '. . . just one of those things you kept making up to keep the void out just another of those old tales to keep the void from pouring in on top of you the shroud.' Later he adds: 'gave up for good and let it in and nothing the worse a great shroud billowing in all over you on top of you and little or nothing the worse little or nothing.' See Samuel Beckett, *That Time,* London: Faber 1976, 11 and 16.

CHAPTER 3 (pp. 27—38)

1 Jacqueline Hoefer's essay, 'Watt', in *Perspective,* vol. ii, No. 3 (Autumn, 1959), 166—82, is cited and endorsed by Kenner, *Samuel Beckett: A Critical Study,* 58, n. 7. Cohn presses the point a little further, treating Watt as a rationalist in an irrational world. See her *Back to Beckett,* 42. Similarly, Schultz argues that 'Watt tries his hand at ordering the world at large.' See *This Hell of Stories,* 21. To this group should be added Robinson, *The Long Sonata of the Dead,* 122—3.

2 Justus Hartnack, *Wittgenstein and Modern Philosophy,* trans. Maurice Cranston, New York: Doubleday 1965, 47.

3 See Olga Bernal, 'Le Glissement hors du langage', in *L'Herne Beckett,* 219—25; and Saint-Martin, *Samuel Beckett et l'Univers de la Fiction,* 7—27.

4 Bernal, 224 [my translation].

5 Samuel Beckett, *Watt,* New York: Grove 1959, 21. Future references to *Watt* will be included in the text with appropriate page number(s) in parentheses.

6 Ruby Cohn has noticed this mirror relationship. See her *Back to Beckett,* 54.

CHAPTER 4 (pp. 39–53)

1 *Mercier and Camier,* trans. Samuel Beckett, 7. All quotations are from the Grove 1974 edition.

2 Samuel Beckett, 'Henri Hayden, homme-peintre', *Documents* (no. 22, 1955), reprinted in *L'Herne Beckett,* 74.

3 Dante, *The Divine Comedy, 2: Purgatorio,* trans. John D. Sinclair, New York: Galaxy 1961. All other quotations from Dante are taken from Sinclair's translation of this work, the *Inferno,* and the *Paradiso.* Since Sinclair's prose translation cannot always be perfectly matched with the corresponding lines of the Italian text, I have restricted myself to citing directly the specific Cantos under discussion. The reader will have no difficulty determining which book of the Divine Comedy is under discussion, if he remembers that the numbering of the Circles belongs to Hell and that of Terraces to Purgatory.

4 From this point of view, it is hard to agree with Raymond Federman's contention that Camier's rejection of Mr Conaire symbolises the rejection of fictional realism. See his *Journey to Chaos,* 164.

5 'Dante . . . Bruno. Vico . . Joyce', in Samuel Beckett and Others, *Our Exagmination Round his Factification for Incamination of Work in Progress,* London: Faber 1972, 22.

6 'The End', trans. Samuel Beckett in *Stories and Texts for Nothing,* 62. Ruby Cohn has also noted this connection. See her *Back to Beckett,* 66.

7 The connection with Belacqua is by no means an innovation in Beckett criticism. Much of the groundwork was done by Walter A. Strauss in his article, 'Dante's Belacqua and Beckett's Tramps', *Comparative Literature,* II (Summer, 1959), 250–261. We can note here that Belacqua's bowed posture recurs throughout Beckett's fiction whenever the narrator incarnates himself. We meet it once in *Mercier and Camier* with Mr Madden: 'Mercier, whose back was to the engine, saw him as he stood there, dead to the passengers hastening towards the exit, bow down his head till it lay on his hands at rest on the knob of his stick' (p. 40).

8 E. M. Cioran, 'Quelques Rencontres', in *l'Herne Beckett*, 104.

CHAPTER 5 (pp. 54—71)

1 This preliminary point has been recognised by many critics. See, for example, Dieter Wellershoff, 'Toujours moins, presque rien', trans. from the German by R. Denturck in *l'Herne Beckett*, 177.

2 There is plenty of evidence that the narrator cannot find a beginning to his long list of stories. Neither Malone nor Molloy, two of his mouthpieces, can remember the provenance of their respective stories or, what amounts to the same thing, how they were brought to the beds from which they start speaking. Moreover, The Unnamable confesses: '. . . it's stories still, or it was never stories, always any old thing, for as long as you can remember, no, longer than that. . .' (p. 385).

3 Hamlet does this admirably. After the tumult of Gertrude's death, Laertes' confession, Claudius' murder, and his own poisoning, Hamlet, in his last words, restores calm: 'The rest is silence.' See *Hamlet*, V, ii, ll. 366—372.

4 Mahood, under the prompting of The Unnamable, alters a schoolroom lesson to emphasise the animal in 'rational animal': 'Pupil Mahood, repeat after me, Man is a higher mammal' (p. 337).

5 Will must be distinguished from appetite which only concerns bodily needs and desires. Beckettian Man has no appetite, as we see as early as Moran: 'For several days I had eaten nothing. I could probably have found blackberries and mushrooms, but I had no wish for them' (p. 162).

6 Reason can only determine truth if it has material to work on. Malone carelessly quotes the dictum of St Thomas Aquinas, 'Nihil in intellectu, etc.' (p. 218). Nothing is found in the human intellect that is not first in the senses. A species, of course, has no senses; only individuals do. Hence, where there is no sensation, there is no knowledge.

7 The evidence is quite clear that fear here is the last reflex

of reason. Very early the narrator states: 'Yes, night was gathering, but the man was innocent, greatly innocent, he had nothing to fear, though he went in fear, he had nothing to fear, there was nothing they could do to him, or very little. But he can't have known it. I wouldn't know it myself, if I thought about it. Yes, he saw himself threatened his body threatened, his reason threatened, and perhaps he was, perhaps they were, in spite of his innocence' (p. 10). When we remember that 'they' also means 'words', we see how the fear is wholly of reason; for the words carry body away in *Malone Dies,* leaving reason to fend alone.

8 Criticism has often assumed that solipsism is alive and well in the Trilogy. For a typical account see Copeland, *Art and the Artist in the Works of Samuel Beckett,* 161–177.

9 I cannot prove it, but Beckett's repeated use of the word, 'inexistence', both in the Trilogy and elsewhere may derive from Brentano's invention of the term to describe the 'intentional' or, as the layman would say, 'mental' being that an object enjoys in the mind of the subject thinking or perceiving it. Conventionally, the idea, 'species', does 'inexist' (this is Brentano's word) in the mind thinking it. Beckett, then, has freed the idea from the individual minds responsible for it, giving it a phenomenological liberty.

10 Maynard Mack, 'The Jacobean Shakespeare' in *Stratford-upon-Avon Studies: Jacobean Theatre,* vol. 1, eds John Russell Brown and Bernard Harris, London: Edward Arnold Ltd 1960, 39.

CHAPTER 6 (pp. 72–82)

1 *Texts for Nothing* was first published as *Textes pour rien* in *Nouvelles et Textes pour rien,* Paris: Editions de Minuit 1955.

2 Samuel Beckett, 'Three Dialogues with Georges Duthuit', in *Proust and Three Dialogues with Georges Duthuit,* London: Calder 1965, 125.

3 'Peintres de l'empêchement' was first published in *Derrière*

le Miroir, Nos 11—12 (1948), 3, 4 & 7., It has been re-published in *l'Herne Beckett,* eds. Tom Bishop and Raymond Federman, 67—70.

4 'Peintres de l'empêchement' in *l'Herne Beckett,* 69.

5 *Ibid,* 69 [my translation].

6 Aristotle, *Metaphysics,* IX, 1051ᵇ 31—33, trans. W. D. Ross.

7 The terms Being and Nothing have been very helpful to other critics of *Texts for Nothing,* but in every case the two words are used in only a general or suggestive way. Ruby Cohn in *Back to Beckett,* 225, speaks of 'Being at the edge of nowhere'; Hugh Kenner in *A Reader's Guide to Samuel Beckett,* 119, explains the work as 'fantasies of non-being'. Neither critic attempts formally to separate Being from Nothing or to explore their relationship. John Fletcher in *The Novels of Samuel Beckett,* 169, takes the title more literally and reads the narration as 'a group of words conveying nothing'. He does not pursue the metaphysical implications of this 'nothing'.

8 The most thorough exponent of this view is Copeland in *Art and the Artist in the Works of Samuel Beckett.* For an interesting application of this approach to *Texts for Nothing,* see Fahrenback and Fletcher, 'The "voice of silence": reason, imagination and creative sterility in "Texts for nothing",' *Journal of Beckett Studies,* Winter, 1976, 30—36.

9 *Proust,* 19.

CHAPTER 7 (pp. 83—94)

1 *How It Is,* trans. Samuel Beckett, 141. All quotations are from the Grove 1964 edition.

2 Sir David Ross, *Aristotle,* 5th ed., London: Methuen 1949, 169—170.

3 *Locke's Essay Concerning Human Understanding,* ed. Mary Whiton Calkins, LaSalle, Illinois: Open Court 1905, 247.

4 Etienne Gilson, *History of Christian Philosophy in the Middle Ages,* New York: Random House 1955, 594.

5 Jean-Paul Sartre, *What is Literature?* trans. Bernard

Frechtman, New York: Harper and Row 1965, 212.

6 The hint is rather strong with its use of the Christian term, 'creature': 'but I'll quicken him you wait and see how I can efface myself behind my creatures when the fit take me now my nails' (p. 52). For an expansion of this point into a theological interpretation of *How It Is,* see Onimus, *Beckett,* 102–103.

CHAPTER 8 (pp. 95–105)

1 Samuel Beckett, 'Peintres de l'empêchement'. Reprinted in *L'Herne Beckett,* 67 [my translation].

2 Samuel Beckett, *The Lost Ones,* 7. All quotations are from the 1972 Calder and Boyars edition.

3 Samuel Beckett, 'The Calmative', in *Stories and Texts for Nothing,* 35.

4 'Ping', trans. Samuel Beckett, in *First Love and Other Shorts,* New York: Grove 1974, 66.

5 'Imagination Dead Imagine', in *First Love and Other Shorts,* 66.

6 There are plenty of earlier examples of this technique in the Trilogy. The phrase 'delicious instants' recurs whenever the narrator refers to a brief experience of absence, a brief experience with no content whatever. Consider this instance (Moran to his son): 'Draw the curtains, I said. Delicious instants, before one's eyes get used to the dark' (*Three Novels,* 104).

7 Samuel Beckett, 'Dante . . . Bruno. Vico . . Joyce', in *Our Exagmination Round his Factification for Incamination of Work in Progress,* 6. Beckett revives the notion in *More Pricks than Kicks,* 148: 'Indeed he went so far as to hazard a little paradox on his own account, to the effect that between contraries no alternation was possible.'

8 *Ibid,* 6.

9 *Ibid,* 8.

CHAPTER 9 (pp. 106–117)

1 'The Expelled', in *Stories and Texts for Nothing,* trans. Samuel Beckett, 25. Since in this chapter I am breaking my rule of treating Beckett's prose fiction in chrono-

logical order, the following bibliographical information might be helpful. 'The Expelled' originally appeared in French as 'L'Expulsé' in 1946. It was in fact written after 'The End' which was originally published as 'Suite' in the same year. The third *nouvelle,* 'The Calmative', was written as 'Le Calmant' during the same period. All these predate *Molloy* which appeared in 1951. As for the three stories considered here, 'First Love', written in French as 'Premier Amour' around 1946, was not published until 1970. The English translation appeared three years later. 'Enough' appeared first as 'Assez' in 1966. 'From an Abandoned Work' was published in French as 'D'un Ouvrage Abandonnée' in the collection *Textes-Mortes* in 1967. It also appeared in English in *No's Knife* the same year. I am indebted to *L'Herne Beckett,* (eds Tom Bishop and Raymond Federman), for this information and heartily refer the reader to it.

2 'The End', in *Stories,* 72.

3 'The Calmative', in *Stories,* 27. Henceforth, these three stories will be referred to in the text with the appropriate page number in parentheses.

4 'First Love', in *First Love and Other Shorts,* trans. Samuel Beckett, 23. 'First Love' will be henceforth referred to in the text under the abbreviation, 'Love'.

5 Dante, *Inferno,* trans. John D. Sinclair, 527.

6 The word crops up frequently. Consider these examples: 'I'll tell my story in the past none the less, as though it were a myth . . .' ('The Calmative', 28); '. . . my myth will have it so' ('The End', 71); 'I speak in the present tense, when speaking of the past. It is the mythological present, don't mind it' (*Molloy,* 26).

7 'Enough', in *First Love and Other Shorts,* 57. All future references to 'Enough' will be indicated in the text.

8 Samuel Beckett, *Proust and Three Dialogues with Georges Duthuit,* 126.

9 'From an Abandoned Work' in *First Love and Other Shorts,* 39. All future references to this work will appear in the text.

10 'Afar a Bird', in *For To End Yet Again,* trans. Samuel Beckett, London: Calder 1976, 40–41.

11 *Texts for Nothing*, 101.

CHAPTER 10 (pp. 118–124)

1 Samuel Beckett, *For To End Yet Again and Other Fizzles*, 27. All quotations are from the 1976 Calder and Boyars edition.

2 Echoes of Beckett's essay, 'Peintres de l'empêchement', abound also in 'The Calmative'. We find intact the familiar words, 'no trace', while the forest in which the narrator wanders recalls the conditions of isolation, enclosure, and empty illuminations: 'Yes, no matter where you stood, in this little wood, and were it in the furthest recesses of its poor secrecies, you saw on every hand the gleam of this pale light, promise of God knows what fatuous eternity' ('The Calmative', 28–29).

3 The same temporal device appears in 'Still'. By looking, in this Fizzle, at the persona looking at nothing, the narrator contemplates an image of himself witnessing Nothing. Then, by discovering in that 'still' image a whole succession of tiny movements, he places the persona firmly in time and so again manages to serialise the experience of Nothing.

4 For an excellent discussion of the place of music in Beckett's art see Mercier, *Beckett/Beckett*, 113–117 and 149–159.

5 E. M. Cioran, 'Quelques Rencontres', in *L'Herne Beckett*, 104.

CONCLUSION (pp. 125–128)

1 Cleanth Brooks and Robert Penn Warren, *Understanding Fiction*, 3rd ed., Englewood Cliffs, N.J.: Prentice-Hall, 293.

2 Sartre, *What is Literature*, trans. Frechtman, 39.

Select Bibliography

I. Selected chronology of Beckett's published prose fiction
Where the Beckettian texts used in this study are not the original English editions, they will be indicated by the abbreviation, 'rpt'. For a complete list of all Beckett's publications, including plays for theatre, radio, and television, poetry, critical writings, and translations of other writers, see Raymond Federman and John Fletcher, *Samuel Beckett: His Works and his Critics* (Berkeley: University of California Press, 1970) and Tom Bishop and Raymond Federman, *L'Herne Beckett* (Paris: Editions de l'Herne, 1976).

1934 *More Pricks than Kicks,* London: Chatto and Windus; rpt. London Pan Books Ltd, 1974.

1938 Written in 1935. *Murphy,* London: Routledge; rpt. New York: Grove Press, Inc., 1957.

1951 Written in 1947—1949. *Molloy,* Paris: Editions de Minuit. Translated into English by Patrick Bowles in collaboration with the author, Paris: Olympia Press, 1955 and New York: Grove Press, 1955; rpt. in *Three Novels,* New York: Grove Press, 1965, 7—176.

1953 Written in 1947—1949. *Malone Meurt,* Paris: Editions de Minuit. English trans. *Malone Dies,* New York: Grove Press, 1956; rpt. in *Three Novels,* 179—288.

1953 Written in 1947—1949. *L'Innommable,* Paris: Editions de Minuit. English trans. *The Unnamable,* New York: Grove Press, 1958; rpt. in *Three Novels,* 291—414.

1953 Written in 1942—1945. *Watt,* Paris: Olypmia Press; rpt. New York: Grove Press, 1959.

1955 Written in 1945—1950. *Nouvelles et Textes pour rien,* Paris: Editions de Minuit, 1955. English trans. with

Richard Seaver, *Stories and Texts for Nothing*, New York: Grove Press, 1967.

1957 'From an Abandoned Work', *Evergreen Review*, vol. 1, No. 3, 83—91; rpt. in *First Love and Other Shorts*, New York: Grove Press, 1974, 37—49.

1961 Written in 1960. *Comment C'est*, Paris: Editions de Minuit. English trans. *How It Is*, London: Calder, 1964; rpt. New York: Grove Press, 1964.

1965 *Imagination morte imaginez*, Paris: Editions de Minuit. English trans. 'Imagination Dead Imagine', London: Calder, 1966; rpt. in *First Love and Other Shorts*, New York: Grove Press, 1974, 63—66.

1966 *Assez*, Paris: Editions de Minuit. English trans. 'Enough' in *No's Knife*, London: Calder, 1967; rpt. in *First Love and Other Shorts*, New York: Grove Press, 1974, 53—60.

1966 *Bing*, Paris: Editions de Minuit. English trans. 'Ping', in *No's Knife*, London: Calder, 1967; rpt. in *First Love and Other Shorts*, New York: Grove Press, 1974, 69—72.

1969 *Sans*, Paris: Editions de Minuit. English trans. *Lessness*, London: Calder, 1970.

1970 Written in 1945. *Premier Amour*, Paris: Editions de Minuit. English trans. 'First Love', London: Calder, 1973; rpt. in *First Love and Other Shorts*, New York: Grove Press, 1974. 11—36.

1970 Written in 1945. *Mercier et Camier*, Paris: Editions de Minuit. English trans. *Mercier and Camier*, London: Calder and Boyars, 1974; rpt. New York: Grove Press, 1975.

1970 Written in 1966. *Le Dépeupleur*, Paris: Editions de Minuit. English trans. *The Lost Ones*, London: Calder and Boyars, 1972.

1976 *Pour finir encore et autres foirades*, Paris: Editions de Minuit. English trans. *For to End Yet Again and other Fizzles*, London: Calder and Boyars, 1976.

1978 'All Strange Away', *Journal of Beckett Studies*, Summer 1978, No. 3, 1—9.

II. Critical Studies of Beckett cited in the text

Bernard, G. C., *Samuel Beckett: A New Approach,* New York: Dodd, Mead, 1970.

Bishop, Tom, and Raymond Federman, eds, *L'Herne Beckett,* Paris: Editions de l'Herne, 1976.

Bonnefoi, Geneviève, 'Textes Pour Rien?' *Lettres Nouvelles,* 36 (March, 1956), 424—430.

Cohn, Ruby, *Back to Beckett,* Princeton: Princeton University Press, 1973.

Copeland, Hannah C., *Art and the Artist in the Works of Samuel Beckett,* The Hague: Mouton, 1975.

Esslin, Martin, ed., *Samuel Beckett: A Collection of Critical Essays,* Englewood Cliffs, N.J.: Prentice-Hall, 1965.

Fahrenback, Hannelore and Fletcher, John, 'The "voice of silence": reason, imagination and creative sterility in "Texts for Nothing".' *Journal of Beckett Studies,* Winter 1976, 30—36.

Federman, Raymond, *Journey to Chaos,* Berkeley: University of California Press, 1965.

Fletcher, John, *The Novels of Samuel Beckett,* London: Chatto, 1964.

Hamilton, Alice and Kenneth, *Condemned to Life: The World of Samuel Beckett,* Grand Rapids, Michigan: Eerdmans, 1976.

Hassan, Ihab, *The Literature of Silence,* New York: Alfred A. Knopf, 1967.

Hesla, David, *The Shape of Chaos: An Interpretation of the Art of Samuel Beckett,* Minneapolis: The University of Minnesota Press, 1971.

Hoefer, Jacqueline, 'Watt', *Perspective,* vol. ii, No. 2 (Autumn, 1959), 166—182.

Kenner, Hugh, *Samuel Beckett: A Critical Study,* New York: Grove, 1961.

Kenner, Hugh, *A Reader's Guide to Samuel Beckett,* London: Thames and Hudson, 1973.

Mercier, Vivian, *Beckett/Beckett,* New York: Oxford University Press, 1977.

Onimus, Jean, *Beckett,* Bruges: Desclée de Brouwer, 1967.

Robinson, Michael, *The Long Sonata of the Dead: A Study of Samuel Beckett,* London: Rupert Hart-Davis, 1969.

Saint-Martin, Fernande, *Samuel Beckett et l'Univers de la Fiction,* Montréal: Les Presses de l'Université de Montréal, 1976.

Schultz, Hans-Joachim, *This Hell of Stories: An Hegelian Approach to the Novels of Samuel Beckett,* The Hague: Mouton, 1973.

Strauss, Walter A. 'Dante's Belacqua and Beckett's Tramps', *Comparative Literature,* II (Summer, 1959), 250—261.

Webb, Eugene, *Samuel Beckett: A Study of his Novels,* London: Peter Owen, 1970.

INDEX